# CELEBRATE JESUS

D1408311

by

## Marilyn Senterfitt

### illustrated by Darcy Tom

Music by Helen Friesen, Lucille Golphenee

Cover by Dan Grossmann

Shining Star Publications, Copyright © 1988
A Division of Good Apple, Inc.

ISBN No. 0-86653-425-3

Standardized Subject Code TA ac

Printing No. 987

Shining Star Publications
A Division of Good Apple, Inc.
Box 299
Carthage, IL 62321-0299

Unless otherwise indicated, the King James Version of the Bible was used in preparing the activities in this book.

# DEDICATION

This book is dedicated with love to all the children who have touched my life and so enriched my Christian journey.

SS845

# A WORD TO PARENTS & TEACHERS

The dictionary defines teaching as the imparting of knowledge on a given subject. This book was written for you, the parent/teacher. The subject is Jesus Christ, and the material in it is presented as a tool for you to use in bringing the knowledge of God's Son to children.

The life of Jesus as found in the Gospels is chronologically covered in the twelve chapters of this book. The first page of each chapter is a coloring picture which can be used by the children to compile a book. The second page is a puzzle or quiz that can be used for reviewing material. The last page of each chapter is especially for the parent/teacher. Included are tips, encouragements and suggested activities related to Jesus, which are not covered elsewhere. In between are individual and group activities such as choral readings, creative writing, games, puppet plays, flannel graphs, bulletin boards that teach and much, much more. The goal of every activity is to share Jesus in a joyous and meaningful way.

When the early pioneers traveled to the western frontier, they sometimes carried seed corn. This was as precious to them as fresh water and food. That corn represented the beginning of their first crop in the new land. From it would spring life for generations to come. You as a teacher/parent are encouraged to approach this book as "seed corn." May it serve as a beginning for you that in time may bear fruit in your own creative ideas and planning. The result will be that the children will come to a knowledge of Jesus Christ, and you will be both a better teacher and parent.

Shining Star Publications, Copyright © 1988, A division of Good Apple, Inc.                    SS845

# TABLE OF CONTENTS

# SONGS

# CHORAL READINGS

Shining Star Publications, Copyright © 1988, A division of Good Apple, Inc.

SS845

# BIRTH TO BOYHOOD

On a star-bright night, Jesus was born. His cradle was not found in a majestic palace; instead He slept in a humble stable in a manger filled with hay. It was just what God had planned. Mary and Joseph loved God's Son and cared for Him in every way. From a tiny baby to a young boy, Jesus grew in wisdom and stature and in favor with God and man. This was the beginning of the most wonderful life ever lived!

SS845

# JESUS' FAMILY TREE

In the first chapter of Matthew, there is a genealogy of Jesus Christ. It is a list of the people in Jesus' family. Twenty-four of those names are on this tree. Some will be very familiar to you. They can be found going up, down, across and backward. Circle each as you find it.

**JECHONIAS**
**AMINADAB**
**ABRAHAM**
**SOLOMON**
**ELIAKIM**
**ELEAZAR**
**JOSEPH**
**SALMON**
**THAMAR**
**DAVID**
**ISAAC**
**JACOB**

**JESSE**
**SADOC**
**OZIAS**
**ELIUD**
**ZARA**
**ABIA**
**OBED**
**MARY**
**AMON**
**BOAZ**
**RUTH**
**ASA**

```
              E R
            A L O C U G
          O Z I A S E S U M
        R E U L M N A S A I C
      R I T U C D A V I D L E A M
    M P C I Z A O B L I O M E J O R
    P S E L E A Z A R J E C H O N I A S
    N O M L A S I R A M E N C U Z A R A
    I L O J O S E P H I S E R J A C O B
    R O B E D I M E A R L R U T O N E
    A M I S E A R A M I N A D A B E
    O I S A A C I N U C M R B E S
    N H E L I A K I M E A R I T U
      A D I M C P A R H R A
      L J I O T E R U T H L
          C N E R Y A
```

SS845

# JESUS' BIRTH

## Choral Reading

by

Lucille Golphenee

**BOYS:** Many long years ago, Jesus came down
And was born as a baby, in Bethlehem town.

**GIRLS:** The stars in the heavens shone brightly that night,
As they twinkled and blinked at the wonderful sight.

**BOYS:** Mary, His mother, and Joseph had come
Their taxes to pay—which must surely be done.

**GIRLS:** No room was there found for the Lord at the inn—
The Saviour of earth, the Redeemer for sin.
So He slept with the cattle, a manger His bed
As He lay down in peace His dear little head.

**BOYS:** And shepherds there were in the country nearby,
When the glory of heaven shone down from the sky.
Then they trembled and shook with fear and with dread;
But the angel of God came upon them and said,

**GIRLS:** "Fear not, for I bring you glad tidings of joy;
For in Bethlehem town is a new baby boy:
The Messiah, foretold both by tongue and by pen;
Redeemer for all, and the Saviour of men.
And this be your sign: you shall find the wee stranger
In swaddling clothes wrapped, and His bed is a manger."

**BOYS:** Then came a great host of bright angels, to say,

**GIRLS:** "All glory to God and on earth, peace—today!"

**BOYS:** When the angels were gone, the shepherds all went
To see the new King, who from Heaven was sent.

**GIRLS:** And when they had found Him, they told it abroad.
So joyful were they, and gave praises to God.

**BOYS:** There came from the east three wise men, afar
To see the new King, and they followed His star.

**GIRLS:** Frankincense and myrrh and gold they did bring
And gave to Him there, as they worshipped the King.

SS845

# WRAPPED IN SWADDLING CLOTHES AND LYING IN A MANGER

Luke 2:7 says that Mary "brought forth her firstborn son, and wrapped him in swaddling clothes, and laid him in a manger . . . ." The following activities will help children better understand what a manger and swaddling clothes are.

## SWADDLING CLOTHES

Newborn infants were once wrapped (swaddled) in a long cloth strip to prevent movement. To demonstrate swaddling to your class, you will need a ten-inch doll and one yard of soft white flannel. Cut half of cloth into an 18-inch square and the remainder into four 4½" x 18" strips. Sew the strips together end to end, making one long swathing band.

Lay the doll diagonally on the square with its arms down. Turn the corner above the head back and bring the opposite corner over the feet, as illustrated. Fold other two corners over. Lay one end of long strip over the front of the doll and begin wrapping around the body. Continue over the feet and tuck in free end of strip. Practice several times.

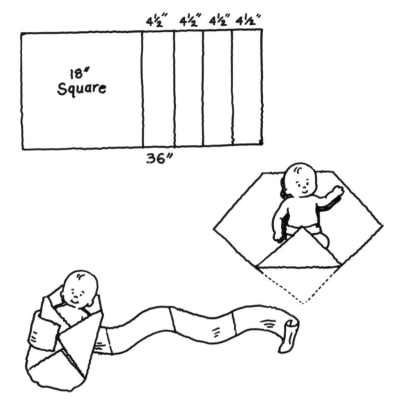

## THE MANGER

A manger is a long, open box used to hold feed for animals in a stable. To make a manger, you will need heavy cardboard or poster board. Using the measurements given here, draw patterns from figures A and B. To "build" the manger, slip slits AB and CD through the slits in the end pieces of the manger. If your swaddled doll is not too heavy, it can lie in the manger. Use Easter grass or dried grass for hay.

This pattern may be used by the children to make individual mangers. Reduce all measurements by half if you wish. Provide grass to use as hay, and let each child shape a baby from modeling clay; or use a small doll.

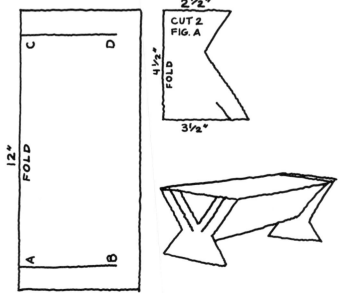

SS845

# SHEPHERDS AND ANGELS
## A SHEPHERD SEARCH

MATERIALS:
Pipe cleaners; 7 small paper squares; colorful string.

DIRECTIONS:
Shape pipe cleaners into shepherds' crooks. Write the following Scripture references on the small pieces of paper and attach with string to crooks: Luke 2:8, 2:9, 2:15, 2:16, 2:17, 2:18, and 2:20. Hide staffs in room and tell pupils to search for them. When all seven are found, have children look up the verses and read them aloud in order.

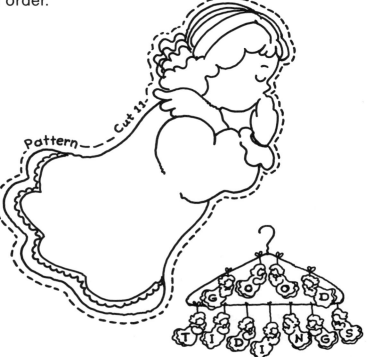

## ANGEL MOBILE

MATERIALS:
White paper; gold glitter; glue; coat hangers; red and green yarn.

DIRECTIONS:
Instruct pupils to cut out 11 angels, using the pattern. Print one letter of the words GOOD TIDINGS on each angel. Have children wrap hangers with green yarn. Make hole in top of each angel and attach to the hanger, using different lengths of red yarn, being sure that GOOD TIDINGS is in the correct order.

## SHEPHERD AND ANGEL TREE

MATERIALS:
Living evergreen tree or spray-painted branch in container; white paper; cotton balls; glue; white yarn.

DIRECTIONS:
Have pupils cut out lambs from pattern. Pull the cotton balls apart and glue cotton on lambs. With a hole punch, make hole in top of each lamb, attach a loop of white yarn and hang on tree. Add several shepherd crooks and angels. The tree may be used in class, or it may be shared with shut-ins or others whose Christmas spirits need a lift.

SS845

# SHARING THE SCRIPTURES

The wise men brought gifts to the Christ Child. Remind children of this as you work together on this recipe for Scripture cake. You may wish to bake the cake as a class project, either in the church kitchen or in a home. Emphasize that the cake is not completely done until it is shared. Provide foil and red and green ribbon with which to wrap the cake slices. The children may use the gift tags shown here as patterns. Help the pupils decide how to share their Scripture cake—with shut-ins, the elderly, the sick, a new neighbor, etc.

Write the recipe on poster board or on a large sheet of paper. Have the class look up verses in a King James Bible. Fill in the spaces as each ingredient is found.

| | | | | |
|---|---|---|---|---|
| 2½ C | f | — — — — | | I Kings 4:22 |
| ½ C | b | — — — — — | | Judges 5:25 (last clause) |
| 1 C | s | — — — — — c — — — | | Jeremiah 6:20 |
| 1 C | r | — — — — — — | | I Samuel 30:12 |
| 1 C | a | — — — — — — — | | Numbers 17:8 |
| 1 T | h | — — — — — | | Proverbs 24:13 |
| 1 t | s | — — — | | Leviticus 2:13 |
| 3 | e | — — — | | Jeremiah 17:11 |
| ¼ C | m | — — — | | Judges 4:19 (last sentence) |
| 1 T | l | — — — — — — | | Amos 4:5 |
| Season with | s | — — — — — — | | II Chronicles 9:9 |

SOLUTION:
flour, butter, sweet cane (sugar), raisins, almonds, honey, salt, eggs, milk, leaven (baking powder), spices (cinnamon, nutmeg, cloves, etc.)

DIRECTIONS:
Preheat oven at 350°. Grease and flour large loaf or tube pan. Cream butter and sugar. Add eggs one at a time, beating each before adding. Stir in honey and milk. Sift in half the flour with salt and baking powder. Mix raisins and nuts with remaining flour and the spices. Add this to the first mixture and stir well. Bake 1 hour and test for doneness by inserting a toothpick. If it comes out clean, the Scripture cake is ready to remove from the oven. Cool, slice, wrap and share!

# GIFT TAGS

Glue the tags to red construction paper. Color and punch holes in upper left corner. Carefully cut out each tag and attach to gifts with red or green yarn.

| | | |
|---|---|---|
| o<br>To:<br>From: | o<br>To:<br>From: | o<br>To:<br>From: |
| o<br>To:<br>From: | o<br>To:<br>From: | o<br>To:<br>From: |

SS845

# GUIDING THE WISE MEN

A bright star led the wise men to the newborn King. Children will enjoy making this ornament. You will need a box of cotton swabs, white glue and dark colored construction paper. Provide each pupil with the star pattern and a manger sticker.

Instruct the children to trace the star on their paper. Put a small amount of glue in a container. (A plastic lid works well.) The pupils are to dip the cotton ends of swabs in glue and place them on the outline of the star. A second and third row can be added on the inside of star, as shown. Glue manger sticker in the center.

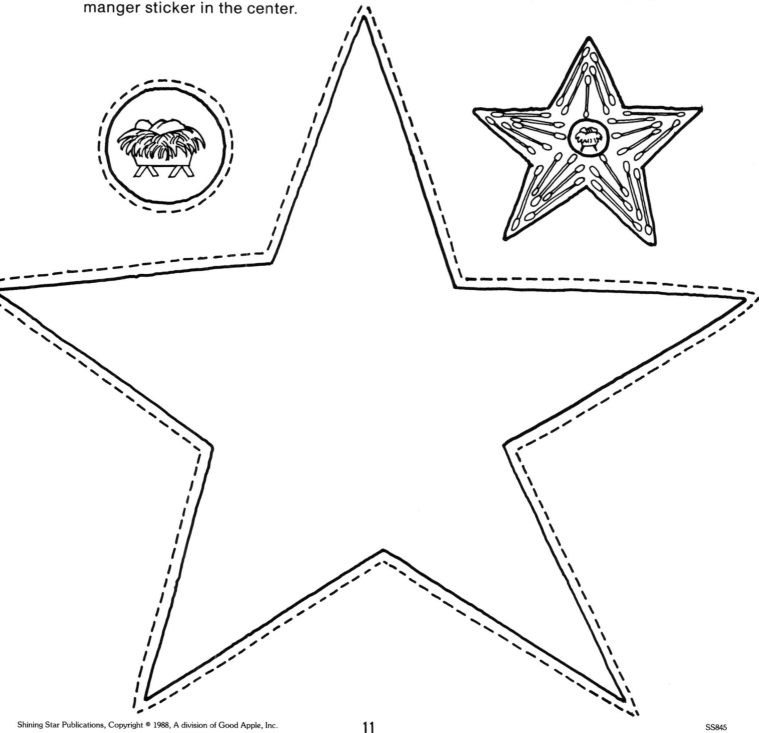

SS845

# BABY JESUS AT CHURCH

In Luke 2:22-40 is the account of infant Jesus being carried to Jerusalem to be presented to the Lord. This simple puppet play requires four puppeteers and one narrator to reenact that event.

**PUPPET STAGE:** Use a cardboard box. Cut away the top, the bottom and one long side, forming a folding, three-sided stage. In the center, cut out a large window. Paste paper columns on either side. You may paint the stage or cover it with fabric. Place at the back edge of a table.

**PUPPETS:** Cut out four finger holders from pattern on page 13. Round the holder on the dotted lines and glue or tape together along sides. Color and cut out Mary with Baby Jesus, Joseph, Simeon and Anna. Attach to the finger holders.

## SCRIPT

**NARRATOR:** Mary and Joseph fulfilled the law by bringing Baby Jesus to the temple in Jerusalem to be presented to the Lord.
(Mary and Joseph enter stage right.)
They brought with them two turtledoves to offer as a sacrifice, according to the law of the Lord. As they stood waiting their turn, a man named Simeon came up to them.

(Simeon enters stage left.)
God had led him to the Temple that day. Simeon had been told he would not see death before he had seen God's promised Son. Simeon was very happy that he was able to see and hold the Christ Child. He left with joy in his heart.

(Simeon exits stage left. Anna enters from the same side.)
A very old woman named Anna approached Mary and Joseph. She served God day and night in the Temple. She, too, knew Baby Jesus' true identity. Anna was overjoyed to be able to see Him. She went quickly to tell everyone the good news.

(Anna exits stage left.)
Mary and Joseph did all the things required to fulfill the law; then they returned to their home in Nazareth.

(Mary and Joseph exit stage right.)
With Mary and Josephs' loving care, Jesus grew to be strong and wise, and the grace of God was upon Him.

Shining Star Publications, Copyright © 1988, A division of Good Apple, Inc.                    SS845

# PUPPET PATTERNS

**MARY HOLDING
JESUS**

**JOSEPH HOLDING
TURTLEDOVES**

**SIMEON**

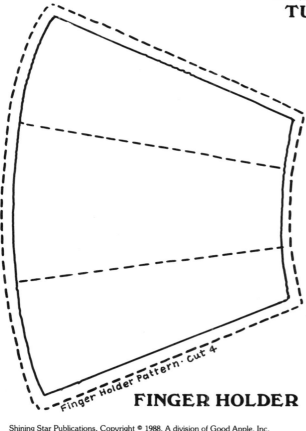

Finger Holder Pattern· Cut 4

**FINGER HOLDER**

**ANNA**

Shining Star Publications, Copyright © 1988, A division of Good Apple, Inc.

SS845

# THE JOURNEY TO EGYPT

God sent an angel, who appeared to Joseph in a dream. He said that wicked Herod would seek to destroy young Jesus, and that Joseph must take Mary and the child to the safety of Egypt. Joseph obeyed, and they left that very night. Joseph must have known his family was finally safe when he sighted the first pyramid that stood tall over the sands of Egypt.

Can you find your way through the maze to the top of this pyramid?

# JESUS AS A BOY

## UNROLL A SCROLL

Share the story of Jesus' visit to the temple at the age of twelve, as found in Luke 2:41-52. Emphasize that Mary and Joseph found Jesus discussing difficult questions with the teachers of the law, and He amazed them with His understanding and answers.

Provide pupils with 5″ or 6″ dowels, glue, and 3″ x 6″ paper cut from brown bags. Instruct them to glue the ends of the paper to the dowels. When dry, gather up the scrolls and print a question covering the birth and boyhood of Jesus on each. Include the Bible reference for each. Roll up the scrolls and tie with string or yarn. Place in a decorated can.

At the next class session, seat the children in a circle. Hold the can and call on a pupil to select a scroll. Have the child read the question aloud and give the answer. If the pupil doesn't answer correctly, read the Bible reference, and ask the other pupils to find the answer in their Bibles. Continue until everyone has had a chance to unroll a scroll.

(This scroll activity may be adapted to cover other areas of Jesus' life.)

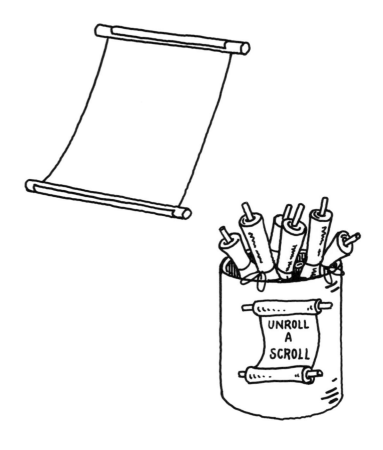

## JESUS GROWS AT HOME

Little is mentioned in the Bible about Jesus' boyhood. We know that He grew strong and wise and was obedient. He also learned carpentry skills from Joseph.

For this activity, cut out seven hammers and seven nails, using the patterns provided. Write the fourteen words of Luke 2:52 on them, alternating a hammer and a nail. Pass them out at random to the class, and instruct each pupil who has a hammer to find the nail containing the next word of the verse.

EXAMPLE:         Favour         with

When the words are in order, ask the children to stand side by side, revealing the entire verse.

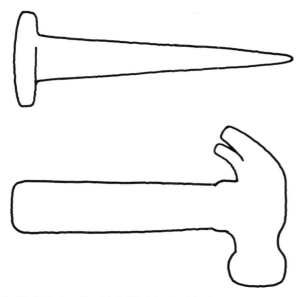

# TEACHING TIPS

## A COLORFUL IDEA

The introductory page of each chapter is to be used as a coloring page. Start a file for each pupil, using a manila folder or a large sheet of paper folded in half. As the children complete each chapter's picture, place it in their file. When all twelve are colored, the pupils may put them together in book form. Provide a hole punch and yarn or a stapler. Attractive covers can be made with wallpaper samples or with two sheets of heavy paper. See coloring sheets on pages: 5, 17, 29, 41, 53, 65, 75, 85, 97, 109, 121, 133.

## THE PLASTIC FANTASTICS

The second page of each chapter is a puzzle or quiz. (See pages 6, 18, 30, 42, 54, 66, 76, 86, 98, 110, 122, 134.) These pages may be used effectively by gluing to lightweight cardboard and covering with clear adhesive-backed plastic. Provide crayons or china markers and a soft cloth or tissue for erasing. The puzzles can thus be used more than once. The puzzles may be put out for use by early arrivers or may be used to review past chapters. Clear plastic can also be applied to mazes, dot-to-dots, or gameboards.

## ART OF RECYCLING

Many activities and projects in this book are designed to be used more than once. You need only to apply a little creative thinking.
FOR EXAMPLE:
Bible Bags, the bulletin board in chapter four, can be used for questioning pupils about any area of Jesus' life. The same is true of the picture patterns, the concentration board, the beanbag game, etc. If something works well with your class, reuse it creatively in other chapter studies.

Shining Star Publications, Copyright © 1988, A division of Good Apple, Inc.

SS845

# PREPARING FOR MINISTRY

At the age of thirty, Jesus began to prepare for His earthly ministry. His baptism in the Jordan River was followed by a mighty confrontation with Satan in the wilderness. Jesus then went about calling the Twelve Disciples. He was committed to following the path God had laid before Him. He went forth prepared to never turn away from that path.

SS845

# REBUS MESSAGE

Solve each rebus by adding or subtracting letters from the words and pictures. Put your answers in the spaces.

---

### THIS MAN BAPTIZED JESUS IN THE JORDAN RIVER.

JOY − Y + 🖐 − AD

_ _ _ _

---

### WHAT DID THE HOLY SPIRIT, SYMBOLIZED AS A DOVE, CALL JESUS?

🐝 − E + 🍀 − CR + D − WRD + 🐛 − AT

_ _ _ _ _ _ _ _ _

---

### JESUS STRUGGLED WITH HIM IN THE WILDERNESS.

SALT − L + 👼 − GEL

_ _ _ _ _

---

### JESUS CALLED THIS NUMBER OF DISCIPLES.

+ ½ − O + EL + 🕊 − DO

_ _ _ _ _ _

---

SS845

**Bulletin Board Idea**

# THE BELOVED SON

This is My beloved Son, in whom I am well pleased.                    Matthew 3:17

OBJECTIVE:  To help children see the qualities in Jesus that they should try to develop in themselves.

MATERIALS:  Cover board with light blue paper or fabric. On a strip of white paper cut out or print the last portion of Matthew 3:17. Center at top of board. If available, use an overhead projector to draw a dove on a large sheet of white paper. The figure of Jesus may be done in the same way, or use an existing picture of Jesus. Cut out both pictures, and place in center of the board, with dove over Jesus' head. Cut out six or more clouds from white paper.

PROCEDURE:  Read together the account of the descending dove, as found in Matthew 3:13-17. Ask the pupils to name qualities in Jesus that would be pleasing to God. Write their answers on the clouds and place around Jesus, as shown. Guide a discussion of how the children could follow Jesus' example and have these qualities in their lives.

SS845

# FLYING DOVES

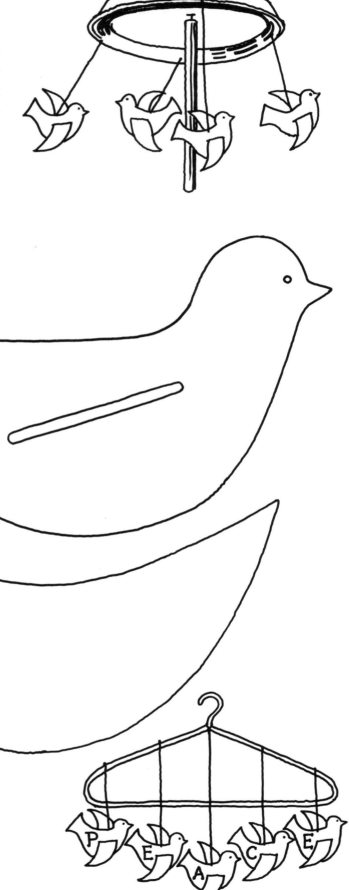

1. Instruct children to cut out four doves, using the patterns found below. They may use poster board, heavy white paper, or Styrofoam trays. Insert wings through slit and secure with tape. Punch four holes equally spaced around an aluminum pie plate. Cut four pieces of yarn, each 8″ long. Insert one end through a hole in the plate, and attach the other end to a dove. Turn the plate upside down and stick a thumbtack through the center, pushing it into a dowel or the eraser end of a pencil. Tell the pupils to rotate the dowel between the palms of their hands, causing the doves to "fly."

2. Have children cut out and assemble five more doves. With a dark crayon or marker, write one letter of the word "peace" on each dove. Attach in order to the coat hanger.

SS845

# THINK! THINK!

# CONCENTRATION GAME

Here is a challenge to pupils' memory and concentration. You will need a 12″ x 24″ bulletin board or hardboard. Place three rows of four pins or small tacks across board, as shown. Punch holes in center top of twelve 3″ x 5″ cards. Print the numbers 1 through 12 on them. On the reverse sides of six cards, print in large letters JESUS, DOVE, DISCIPLES, GOD, JOHN THE BAPTIST, WILDERNESS. Repeat on remaining six cards. Hang cards on board with numbers facing out. The object is to match the six pairs. Call on a pupil to select two numbers. Turn over those cards. If there is no match, turn back over. Tell the children to remember what the cards were and ask a second pupil to call out two numbers. When all six matches have been made, the cards may be moved around, creating a greater challenge for older children.

Any information can be used in this game. The children can match Disciples' names, halves of memory verses, people whom Jesus healed, etc.

SS845

# TEMPTATION IN THE WILDERNESS

Read together Matthew 4:1-11. Discuss the three ways in which Satan tempted Jesus and what Jesus' reply was in each case.

## A FRIEZE IS FUN!

When the children are fully acquainted with the temptation story, provide materials to make a frieze. Divide newsprint or butcher paper into six large sections and hang on wall at pupils' eye level. In sections two, four, and six, write the heading "JESUS SAID," and fill in his replies to the three temptations. Leave spaces one, three, and five for the children to draw their interpretation of the temptations. Let children work in groups, using colored chalk, markers, crayons or paints to complete their drawings. (They may make practice drawings first.)

## THAT IS TEMPTING!

This activity will help the children to better deal with their own temptations. Divide the class into TEMPTERS and RESISTERS. To get things started you may need to provide written temptations for the TEMPTERS to read. The RESISTERS should give an answer in their own words. Guide them to say more than "No, that's wrong," as a reply. Children should try to provide reasoning for their responses. Some temptations might be "Let me copy your homework," "Let's steal that candy bar," or "Did you hear what Mary said about Susie?" Allow time for the TEMPTERS to switch roles and become RESISTERS.

SS845

# THE CHOSEN DOZEN

Jesus called twelve men to be His Disciples and follow Him. Can you identify them from the clues? Their names are listed below.

1. Nicknamed "the rock"  ___ ___ T ___ ___
2. The Beloved  ___ H ___ ___
3. A son of Zebedee  ___ ___ E ___ ___
4. Brother of Peter  ___ D ___ ___ ___
5. A tax collector (publican), also called Matthew  ___ ___ ___ I ___
6. Doubted Jesus' Resurrection  ___ ___ S ___ ___
7. The traitor  ___ ___ ___ ___ ___   ___ ___ C ___ ___ ___ ___ ___
8. Called Zelotes  ___ ___ I ___ ___
9. Brought Nathanael to Jesus  P ___ ___ ___ ___ ___
10. Also named Nathanael  ___ ___ ___ L ___ ___ ___ ___ ___
11. Surname of Lebbaeus  ___ ___ ___ ___ ___ E ___ ___
12. A son of Alphaeus  ___ ___ S ___ ___ ___

# THE TWELVE DISCIPLES

### Words and Music by
### Helen Friesen

When Je-sus did His work be-low, He chose some help-ers to car-ry on.
Mat-thew, the tax col-lec-tor, came, Phil-ip and al-so Bar-thol-o-mew.
Add yet the name of Thad-dae-us, Which means we come to the last of them—

Down at the sea-shore, He called to Pe-ter, An-drew and James and John,
James, son of Alph-aeus, Si-mon, the Zea-lot, Thom-as, the doubt-er, too.
Ju-das Is-car-iot, who be-trayed Je-sus, These were the Mas-ter's men.

# FISHERS OF MEN

When Jesus called the brothers Peter and Andrew, He told them that He would make them fishers of men. Most children are fascinated with magnets and will enjoy the following activity to reinforce the names of the Disciples.

Cut out twenty colorful fish from the pattern. Print the names of the Disciples on some of them and on the rest print the names of people who did not follow Jesus: Herod, Pilate, Satan, Pharisees, Rich Young Ruler, etc. Attach a paper clip to each fish. Scatter on a large blue paper or piece of fabric. Make fishing poles from pencils. Cut a small piece of adhesive-backed magnetic tape and stick to one end of a string. Tie the other end to a pencil.

Give each pupil a "fishing pole" and a plastic sandwich bag. As children begin to fish, explain that the only fish that are "keepers" are those with names of people who followed Jesus. When a child catches a Disciple, he may put it in his bag. Any others must be thrown back into the sea. Children may continue fishing until all the Disciples are "caught."

SS845

# WHO ARE THEY?

## SPELL THE TWELVE

Print the following letters on 3" x 5" cards:
Two each of A, E, I, O, P, S, T, D
One each of B, C, H, J, L, M, N, R, U, W
Using the list found in Matthew 10:2-4, call out a Disciple's name. Ask the children to spell that name. The pupils with the correct letters will stand side by side, showing their letters and spelling the name. You may ask each group of spellers to tell something about their Disciple. Continue until all twelve have been spelled.

## NAME THE TWELVE

Print the names of the Disciples on 4" x 8" strips of paper. You may use the list found in Matthew 10:2-4, in Mark 3:16-19, or in Luke 6:14-16, as mentioned above. As each pupil arrives, pin a name on his/her back. The names can be duplicated for larger classes. Explain to the children that they are to find out which Disciple they are by questioning the other pupils. The questions must have a yes or no answer. After a period of time, call the class to order. Ask who can name his or her Disciple. For those who were not able to identify their Disciple, let the other pupils give clues. They may be very simple. For example: "His name begins with a B and ends with a W."

# SET THE SCENE

Children will be better able to do this activity when they are thoroughly familiar with the events related to Jesus' preparation for His ministry.

PROCEDURE: Reproduce the patterns on pages 26 and 27 and give to pupils. Ask children to color and cut out each figure. Pass out large sheets of paper and glue. Instruct the children to create the background scenery for Jesus' baptism, the temptation in the wilderness, or the calling of the Disciples. Stick figures may be drawn to represent people. If your church has a good supply of teaching pictures, they can be cut up and used along with the patterns provided here.

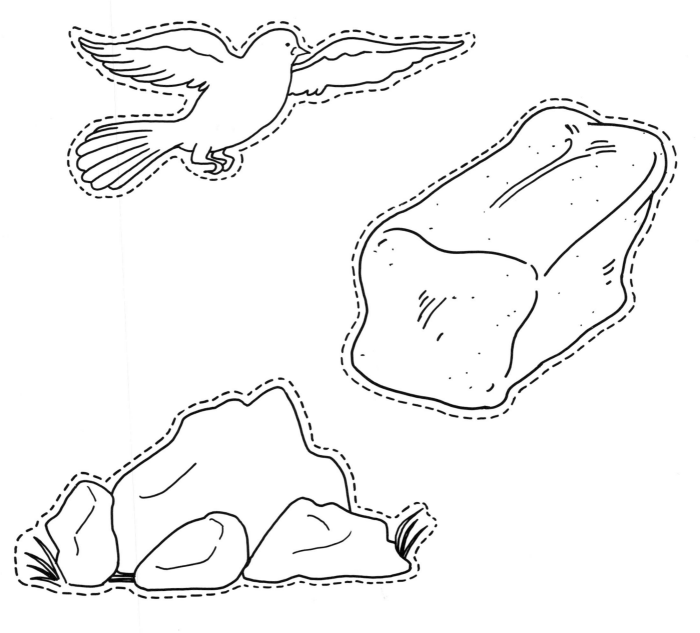

# MORE SET THE SCENE PATTERNS

SS845

# THE FOUR GOSPELS

Our knowledge of the life of Jesus is based primarily on the first books of the New Testament. The children will realize this as they begin to look up stories and verses in their Bibles. The following activities will make them more aware of Matthew, Mark, Luke and John.

## A BANNER TIME

Banners may be made from four 8" x 16" pieces of fabric or paper. You will need four 10" dowels and colorful yarn. Make each banner a different color combination. Glue the top edge of paper or fabric over the dowel and attach yarn as hanger. The bottom may be hemmed. Cut out and glue on letters, or print the name of one Gospel on each banner. Also cut out pictures of scrolls or Bibles and use as shown; or have children design an appropriate symbol for each Disciple. Hang banners together, or place around the classroom.

## WRITE ABOUT IT

Divide class into four groups and assign each group a Gospel. Instruct them to find out all they can about the author of their book, when it was written and its main theme. Provide Bible dictionaries and concordances. The children may take the assignments home and bring their reports to the next class meeting.

## MARKING THE GOSPELS

Place a large Bible on a table in the classroom. Prepare a poster with the heading MARK THE GOSPELS. Select subjects to be marked, and choose a color for each. Example: Jesus heals—red; miracles—blue; parables—orange; etc. Print the color code on the poster and place near the Bible. Cut out strips of paper in the colors chosen. When a subject is covered in class, pupils may find the verses in each Gospel and mark with the strips. Some stories will be in only one book and others will appear in all four.

SS845

# THE MASTER TEACHER

Jesus had a mission to teach the people about God and His heavenly kingdom. He often shared these lessons through stories that both young and old could understand and enjoy. His own dedicated life taught everyone just how God expected them to live. Jesus took every opportunity to teach—on a mountain, by the sea, in the temple or in a home. He was truly the Master Teacher.

SS845

# BLESSED ARE THEY

In the Sermon on the Mount, Jesus taught about those who will be blessed. There is a special word for these special blessings. Complete this puzzle by matching the blessed with the blessing, according to Matthew 5:3-12. Read the letters down and learn what that special word is.

E.  a heavenly reward
I.  shall obtain mercy
E.  shall be comforted
U.  children of God
B.  kingdom of heaven
T.  shall be filled
A.  inherit the earth
D.  kingdom of heaven
T.  shall see God

___ 1. Poor in spirit
___ 2. They shall mourn
___ 3. The meek
___ 4. Hunger and thirst after righteousness
___ 5. The merciful
___ 6. Pure in heart
___ 7. The peacemakers
___ 8. Persecuted for righteousness sake
___ 9. Revile, persecute and say evil against

# THE WOMAN AT THE WELL

Read together John 4:4-30 and 39-42. As a review of the story of the Samaritan woman's encounter with Jesus, prepare the following activity.

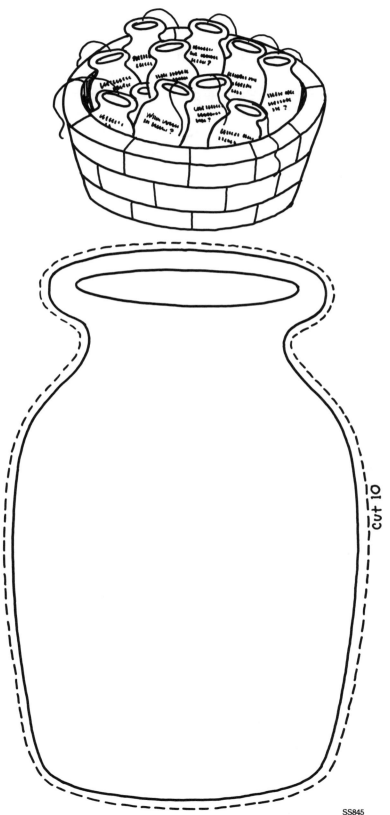

Draw a 10" circle on poster board. Supply clay and have children make blocks of uniform size. Instruct them to make a foundation of 2" blocks around the circle and then build up three or four rows on top of it. Make ten paper jars from the pattern and attach string or yarn to each. Print suggested questions on them and place inside well, with strings hanging over the wall.

Have children take turns drawing out a paper jar and answering the question on it. If they do not know the answer, return the jar to the well and continue until all the questions have been answered correctly.

1. To what country did Jesus say he "must needs go"?

2. Who made the well that Jesus rested upon?

3. What did Jesus ask the Samaritan woman to give Him?

4. Why was the woman surprised that Jesus would speak to her?

5. What kind of water did Jesus offer the woman?

6. Who did the woman say would come and tell all things to the people?

7. What was Jesus' response when the woman said she knew the Messiah would come some day?

8. What did the woman do after the Disciples arrived?

9. How long did Jesus stay in the city of Sychar?

10. What two things caused the people to believe that Jesus was "the Christ, the Saviour of the world"?

cut 10

SS845

# THE MAN IN THE TREE

The story of Zacchaeus is one of the most popular with children. This stick-puppet skit will be met with enthusiasm.

MATERIALS: Four 12" dowels, a cardboard box, heavyweight paper.

PROCEDURE: Reproduce patterns on pages 32 and 33. Glue to heavyweight paper. Color and cut out. Attach each at the end of dowel. Cut top and one side from box. Cut out a large tree and glue on stage left, or secure a tree branch in clay. Blue sky and clouds may be added to the background.

SKIT: Two pupils may control the four puppets. One will handle the two Zacchaeus figures; the other, Jesus and the crowd. Use a narrator to tell the story (see page 34) while it is acted out by the puppeteers.

SS845

# SCRIPT

Jesus entered the city of Jericho.
(Move Jesus to stage right.)

He was followed by a great crowd.
(Move crowd in front of Jesus so that only His head can be seen.)

A man named Zacchaeus lived in Jericho. He was curious about Jesus and wanted to see Him.
(Move Zacchaeus to left of crowd.)

Zacchaeus was not well liked because he had become rich by overtaxing the people! Zacchaeus was not very tall, and the crowd refused to move aside so that he, too, could see Jesus.
(Move Zacchaeus up and down as if he is trying to see over crowd.)

A tall sycamore tree stood nearby. It gave Zacchaeus a bright idea. He climbed the tree and sat on a limb.
(Move the standing Zacchaeus up the tree and replace with the sitting figure.)

Jesus and the crowd moved closer to the tree. Suddenly Jesus looked up.
(Position Jesus in front of the crowd at the base of the tree.)

Jesus: "Zacchaeus, make haste and come down; for today I must abide in thy house." Zacchaeus was so startled that Jesus knew his name that he nearly fell out of the tree! He joyfully came down and led Jesus to his home.

(Move Zacchaeus down tree and replace with standing figure, in front of Jesus. Remove both figures to stage left.)

The crowd was upset with Jesus and murmured that He should not go to the home of such a terrible sinner. They went away in anger.
(Remove crowd. Place Zacchaeus and Jesus stage center.)

Zacchaeus had a pleasant dinner and a very rewarding talk with Jesus.
Zacchaeus: "Behold, Lord, the half of my goods I give to the poor; and if I have taken any thing from any man by false accusation, I restore him fourfold."
Jesus was pleased with Zacchaeus' declaration. He bade him a warm farewell and continued His journey.
(Remove Jesus stage left.)

Zacchaeus never forgot his visit with Jesus, and he lived the rest of his days just as Jesus had taught him.
(Remove Zacchaeus.)

# JESUS BLESSES THE CHILDREN
## Choral Reading   by Lucille Golphenee

The presentation of this choral reading requires three groups: Mothers, Disciples and Children. One pupil will say the words of Jesus. Set the scene with Jesus sitting center stage. Mothers and Children stand on right of stage and Disciples on left.

(Everyone faces audience.)

ALL:
Jesus loves the little children,
All of them both far and near.
Every race and every color,
They to Him are very dear.
(Mothers and Children move to Jesus, and Children sit at His feet. Disciples move to Jesus from left.)

MOTHER:
Mothers brought their little darlings
For the Lord to bless one day.
Some were there who thought it foolish;
Tried to make them go away.

DISCIPLES:
But the Master's look was tender
As He bless'd each little tot.
And he said to His Disciples,

JESUS:
"Let them come; forbid them not."

CHILDREN:
And the children knew He loved them;
They were not a bit afraid
As the Saviour called them to Him,
Laid His hands on them, and prayed.

DISCIPLES:
His Disciples asked a question
At another time, to see
In the kingdom of His glory,
Who the greatest one should be.
(One child stands by Jesus.)

MOTHERS:
Then the Master looked about Him,
Called to Him a little child;
Pure was he—so sweet and trusting.
Innocent. He sweetly smiled.

JESUS:
Then He said, "If you would enter
Heaven's kingdom by and by,
You must be as little children,
Or you shall not reign on high.
And whoever would be greatest,
Meek and humble must become,
(Pointing to the child before Him.)

Even as this little one."
(Everyone faces audience.)

ALL:
Yes, He loves the little children;
They are precious to His heart.
And if they will only trust Him,
He from them will never depart.

# TWO SISTERS LEARN A LESSON

Jesus often visited Bethany and stayed at the home of Lazarus and his two sisters, Mary and Martha. Read to the children the account of one of those visits (Luke 10:38-42).

## TWO WAYS TO SERVE JESUS

Cut a poster board in half. Put "MARY" at the top of one poster and "MARTHA" at the top of the other. On MARY'S poster draw or glue a picture of someone praying, worshiping in church, etc. On MARTHA'S poster place a picture of someone being a helper, visiting the sick, etc. Ask the children to list on the posters things they can do for Jesus that would be representative of the folded hands of MARY or the busy hands of MARTHA.

## A FUN RECIPE

If Jesus had visited Mary and Martha during Purim, they might have served these sweet treats to Him. Purim is celebrated even today with wonderful foods, especially desserts!

YOU WILL NEED
2 cups rolled oats
¼ cup sugar
3 tablespoons melted butter
3 tablespoons milk
¾ teaspoon almond extract

Use a blender or food processor and grind the oats until very fine. Add the sugar and mix well. Mix together the butter, milk and almond extract. Add oat mixture and stir until all ingredients are combined. Shape into small balls and refrigerate for a few hours.

# A GOOD PLACE TO TEACH

Connect the letters alphabetically and learn where Jesus taught a great crowd.
The answer is found in Mark 4:1.

# THE SECRET FOLLOWER

In the third chapter of John, we meet Nicodemus. This powerful man did not want anyone to know that he was interested in the man called Jesus; so he came to Jesus by night, declaring, "Rabbi, we know that you are a teacher come from God; for no one can do those things that you do, unless God is with him." As a result of this secret meeting, Nicodemus went his way truly knowing Jesus.

Make copies of this "crypto" code and the message below. Instruct children to decipher Jesus' words to Nicodemus—words which changed Nicodemus' life.

A = ∧
E = ∩
I = I
O = O
U = ∪
B = bed
C = car
D = dog
F = fish
G = girl
H = house
J = jug
K = kid
L = lamp
M = mouse
N = nail
P = pot
Q = queen
R = rose
S = snail
T = tie
V = valentine
W = water
X =
Y = you
Z = zebra

Allow time for pupils to form their own coded

Shining Star Publications, Copyright © 1988, A division of Good Apple, Inc.

SS845

# A BEANBAG GAME

Jesus taught thousands of people during His ministry on earth. The clues in this game will help children identify the Samaritan woman, Nicodemus, Mary, Martha, Zacchaeus and the Disciples.

MATERIALS:

Divide a poster board into six equal sections. To make the poster reusable, print the clues below on construction paper and fasten by removable tape to each section. Make a beanbag by sewing two 5″ squares together. Leave a small hole and fill with dried beans or rice. Sew the opening securely shut.

PROCEDURE:

Lay the poster on the floor. Direct pupils to take turns tossing the bag. When they land on a clue, they are to identify the person or persons Jesus taught. If they land on a line, they can try another toss. When the clues have been identified, they may be replaced with six more clues.

This game board may be used to teach or reinforce any information about Jesus.

| | | |
|---|---|---|
| MET JESUS AT A WELL | THE CHOSEN TWELVE | SHE SAT AT JESUS' FEET |
| THE BUSY HOMEMAKER | HE CLIMBED A TREE | A SECRET FOLLOWER |

SS845

# TEACHING TIPS

## AN OBJECTIVE LOOK

The next time you enter your classroom, try to look at it through the eyes of your pupils. The atmosphere of a room can teach. Are your children stimulated by what they see, or is the room drab and dull? Check your room against this list.

Clean and neat
No clutter
Well-lighted
Tables and chairs correct height
Cheerful colors throughout
Marked storage areas
Room to move around
A smiling teacher

If your room is small and you have a limited budget, be creative. You can do amazing things with just a cardboard box! Get as much as you can out of what you have, and remember—the room is for the children, not the teacher.

## FRESH IDEAS

Be alert to new ideas. Dare to try them. Jesus is the best example of a teacher who had something to say and chose to use new methods to reach that goal. His parables were a teaching success. Pray, asking God to make you an enthusiastic and exciting teacher. Do it not only for yourself, but for all those children entrusted to you.

## LEARNING CENTERS

A learning center is a place set aside for self-teaching. It is an effective use for the corner of a room. Younger children may need some guidance, but centers should be self-explanatory, containing some clear and simple directions. Here are a few examples: a tape recording that pupils listen to with earphones; simple projects with materials available; matching games or Bible games; Bible verses to mark.

SS845

# THE GREAT PHYSICIAN

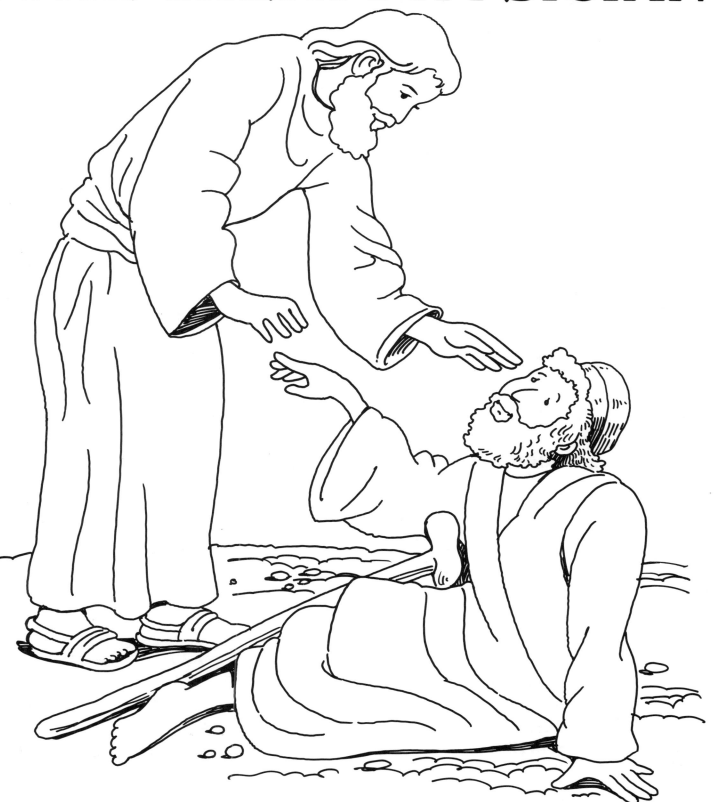

As Jesus traveled from place to place, the blind received their sight, the lame walked, lepers were cleansed, the deaf were given their hearing, the dead were raised up. All these things Jesus did without the help of pills, ointments or surgical tools. Because of His great love, people were healed in mind, in body and in soul.

SS845

# BOUNDING BUTTERFLIES

In the summertime, butterflies flit here and there. These six butterflies carry the names of some very happy people who were healed by Jesus. Read the numbered Scriptures, and then write people's names on the bounding butterflies.

1. Luke 8:41, 42, 49-56
2. Luke 5:12-15
3. Matthew 8:5-13
4. Matthew 20:29-34
5. Mark 2:3-12
6. Matthew 8:14-15

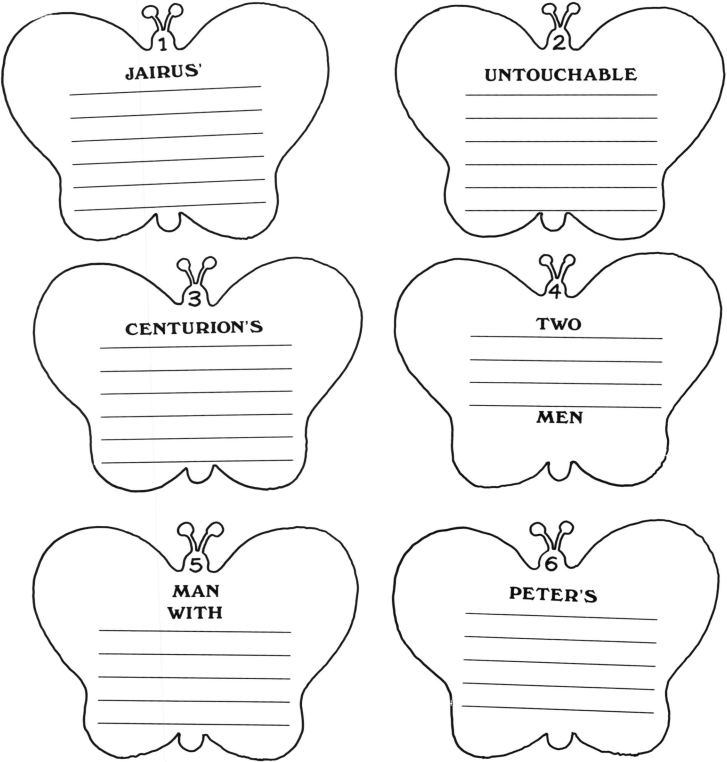

1 JAIRUS'

2 UNTOUCHABLE

3 CENTURION'S

4 TWO ... MEN

5 MAN WITH

6 PETER'S

Shining Star Publications, Copyright © 1988, A division of Good Apple, Inc.

SS845

# BIBLE BAGS

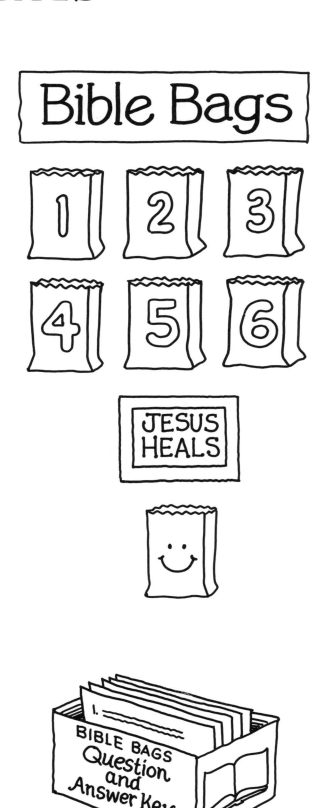

OBJECTIVE:

This bulletin board is an ongoing question-and-answer game. The questions may be based on any subject from the life of Jesus. Use the chapter titles as a guide. This game should create interest in learning about Jesus.

MATERIALS:

Cover the bulletin board with newsprint or a lightweight fabric as a background. Attach lunch-size brown bags to boards. Cut out letters or print the words BIBLE BAGS on a strip of paper and place at center top. Number the bags 1 through 6 and place on the board as shown. Draw a large smiling face on one bag and position at center bottom. On an 8" x 10" piece of construction paper, print the subject matter. Place at center top. Put questions on 3" x 5" cards. Include 3-5 questions in each bag. Make an answer key for yourself and include Bible references for all questions. Prepare a small box for filing cards and answer keys under each subject title. They may then be used for review or with future classes.

PROCEDURE:

Seat the children in front of board. Call on a child to select a question card from a numbered bag. Read the question for younger children. If the child gives the correct answer, she places card in the smiling face bag. If she does not know the answer she may either return the card to the numbered bag or you may give her a Bible reference to find. Continue the game while the child is finding the answer. When the correct answer is given, the card is placed in the smiling face bag. Smiling face stickers may be given to each child who gives a correct answer. Prepare 2" x 10" strips of colored paper. Print SMILE FOR JESUS and child's name at top of each. Hang on the wall. As a child receives a sticker, she may place it on her strip.

# PICTURE PATTERNS

Here is an enjoyable art project that may be done in one of two ways. For younger children, glue the pattern pages (found below and on page 45) to lightweight cardboard. Cut out each figure. Children may trace around them and draw in their own features. For older children reproduce pattern pages for each child. Instruct them to color the figures and then cut them out.

## PROJECT

Give each child a large piece of newsprint or drawing paper with THE GREAT PHYSICIAN printed at the top. Instruct children to create either an indoor or an outdoor setting by tracing or gluing the patterns to the large background paper.

When the background has been completed, have children draw stick figures that depict Jesus healing someone: Peter's mother-in-law, Jairus' daughter, a blind man, the paralyzed man, etc.

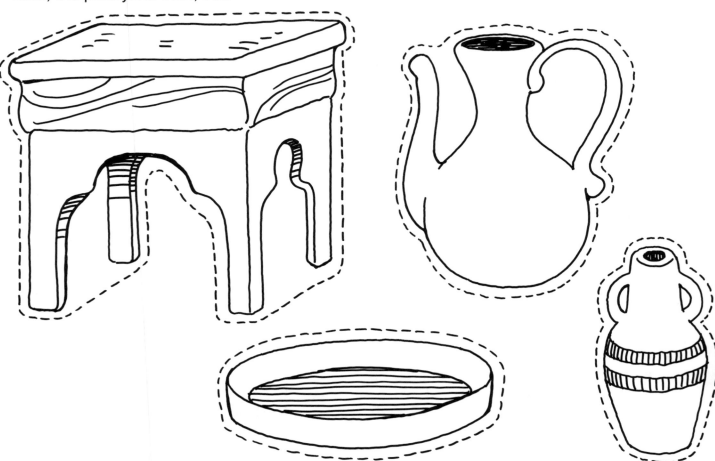

These patterns may also be used to create pictures for other events in Jesus' life. File away for use with future studies.

SS845

# MORE PICTURE PATTERNS

SS845

# PRESCRIPTION FOR LOVE

OBJECTIVE:
Most children have experienced going to the doctor and having medicine prescribed for a cold or other illness. This activity will help children see how Jesus healed the sick in His own special way—by touch, and with just a few words. In some cases He healed someone who was not in his physical presence!

PREPARATION:
Materials include a heavy 22" x 26" poster board, two dozen personal size envelopes, two dozen 3" x 5" cards, strips of white cloth; makeup.

Fold poster board in half. Cut out backs of envelopes, making pockets as shown. Fold flap toward front. Using the envelopes' glue, secure to poster. On twelve cards print in large letters names of persons healed. On reverse side list appropriate reference. On remaining twelve cards print the "prescription" used by Jesus to heal the sick.

Place name cards on left side of table and place "prescription" cards on right side. Stand poster in center of table.

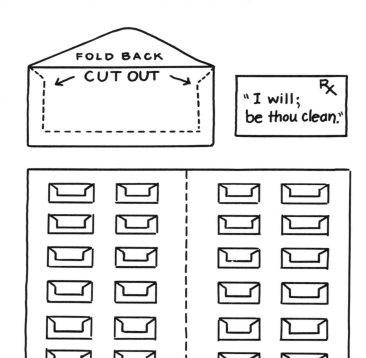

| NAME CARDS | BIBLE VERSES | PRESCRIPTION CARDS |
|---|---|---|
| A Leper | Matthew 8:3 | ". . . I will; be thou clean . . . ." |
| Paralyzed Man | Luke 5:24 | ". . . I say unto thee, Arise, and take up thy couch, and go into thine house." |
| Man with Withered Hand | Mark 3:5 | ". . . Stretch forth thine hand . . . ." |
| Blind Man | John 9:7 | ". . . Go, wash in the pool of Siloam . . . ." |
| Deaf and Dumb | Mark 7:34 | ". . . Ephphatha . . . Be opened." |
| Woman with Crooked Back | Luke 13:12 | ". . . Woman, thou art loosed from thine infirmity." |
| A Demoniac | Mark 1:25 | ". . . Hold thy peace, and come out of him." |
| Jairus' Daughter | Matthew 9:24 | ". . . Give place: for the maid is not dead, but sleepeth . . . ." |
| Nobleman's Son | John 4:50 | ". . . Go thy way; thy son liveth . . . ." |
| High Priest's Servant | Luke 22:51 | ". . . And he touched his ear, and healed him." |
| Thankful Leper | Luke 17:19 | ". . . Arise, go thy way: thy faith hath made thee whole." |
| Peter's Mother-in-Law | Luke 4:39 | "And he stood over her, and rebuked the fever; and it left her . . . ." |

PROCEDURE:
Each child chooses a name card and pantomimes the part of the person listed on that card. Encourage children to be creative in acting out parts. Some ideas are—place hand over ears, mouth or eyes to represent people who are deaf, mute or blind. A white cloth used as a bandage or a sling can dramatize the plight of a leper. A demoniac can cry out; the dead must lie very still and the paralyzed lie down and move only upper body. Peter's mother-in-law can be made up to look feverish. The children may also describe their character to the class in their own words. The class can decide what method Jesus used to heal a particular person and match the name cards, Bible verses and prescription cards. When the matches are made correctly, place cards in side-by-side envelopes on the poster.

The poster board pockets can be used with other information about Jesus. Memory verses can be cut in half and matched. The Disciples' names can be done in the same manner. Store the poster board and use it creatively in future class sessions!

SS845

# HIS MIRACLES

**Words and Music by
Helen Friesen**

## BIBLE STORIES

# SAYING THANK YOU

Share the account of the ten lepers (Luke 17:11-19) with the children. Discuss times when they might not have expressed thanks to someone who helped them. Guide the children in making a list of those they would like to thank: pastor, church staff, family, friends, neighbors, etc.

Provide materials for making cards:

Construction paper folded in half
Yarn
Heavy foil
White glue

For younger children, write "THANK YOU" on face of card. Older children can outline words "THANK YOU" with glue. Set aside to dry. When glue is completely hard, cover with foil, making the words stand out in relief. Or have children place yarn over the letters before glue sets. Place personal messages of thanks inside. Have the children handdeliver cards.

# BEING A FRIEND

Share the story of the "man with eight legs" as recorded in Mark 2:3-12. Ask if the four who carried the sick man were truly friends. Lead a discussion on what it means to be a friend. Emphasize the importance of the involvement of the four friends. If they hadn't taken the paralyzed man to Jesus, he might never have walked. Give each child a copy of the card below and a personal-sized envelope. Ask them to think of those who are absent or ill who they can reach out to in friendship. Instruct them to color the bow, fold as shown and write a cheerful note inside. Provide addresses and postage.

SS845

# BLIND FROM BIRTH

Read together about the healing of the blind man in John 9:1-7. The following activities will help children to experience the world of the sightless and better understand what a joy it would be to see after a lifetime of blindness.

In a cardboard box, place objects of different textures and shapes: a small Bible; a rock; cotton swabs; sandpaper; fruit; etc. Provide a blindfold and let the children take turns identifying an object using only their sense of touch and smell.

Blindfold two children and then move furniture around the room. Ask the children to hold hands and find their way to a predetermined spot in the room. The other pupils may warn them if they are about to trip over something!

# BE OPENED!

Share the account of the deaf and dumb man found in Mark 7:32-37. Help children to realize that dumb does not mean ignorant, but indicates that the man could not speak. The following activities will help children experience how it feels to be unable to speak or hear.

Instruct younger children to place their hands over their ears. Older pupils may put cotton in their ears. Play music for a few minutes or tell a Bible story. Ask class if they were able to understand, and if they felt left out because they could not hear clearly.

Tell class that deaf people often "hear" by reading lips or communicate by using sign language. Select an account of Jesus' healing and act out the story silently. As you go through the motions, tell the story by moving only your lips. Upon completion, ask the pupils what the story was about. Give children an opportunity to share their own silent stories.

SS845

# JESUS BE IN ME

Give each child a copy of this reading. Help them to memorize it. In their study of Jesus as the Great Physician they have learned that He healed many parts of the body. Children should point to each body part as it is mentioned throughout the presentation. Other suggestions for motions have been placed in parentheses after the appropriate lines.

Jesus be in my mouth
To help me speak only the truth.
(Move fingers to represent a mouth talking.)

Jesus be in my ears
To help me hear just the good.
(Hand cupped to ear.)

Jesus be in my eyes
To help me see all the beauty.
(Hand above eyes; peer about.)

Jesus be in my hands
To help me do right with them.
(Simulate building something.)

Jesus be in my legs
To help me walk in your way.
(Step in place.)

Jesus be in my heart
To help me do my very best.

(Stand tall and straight.)

Jesus, please come into my
mouth,
ears,
eyes,
hands,
legs
and heart.

Jesus, my Lord and Saviour,
Come and be in all of me!
(Spread arms to welcome Jesus.)

SS845

# QUESTION AND ANSWER SCOPE

Use a cardboard box approximately 9" x 12" x 2". Cut two 3" x 5" windows in the lid, spaced about 4" apart. Print "Question" above the right opening and "Answer" above the left. With the lid on the box, cut two holes, spaced evenly, on each side, so that dowels can be inserted (see diagram).

On a long strip of newsprint 7" wide, trace pairs of 3" x 5" rectangles matching the spacing of the windows on the box. On each pair of rectangles print a question and an answer, the question being on the left one and the answer on the right. Tape the ends of the strip to the dowels, and roll the entire strip onto the right dowel.

To reveal a question, followed by the answer, rotate the left dowel. The question and answer scope may be used individually or as a class activity.

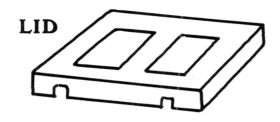

LID

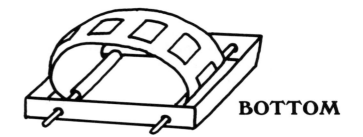

BOTTOM

## SUGGESTED QUESTIONS AND ANSWERS

1. How many lepers returned to say thank you? (one)
2. What did Jesus heal on the servant of the high priest? (his ear)
3. Who asked Jesus to heal his daughter? (Jarius)
4. How did Jesus heal the blind man by the pool? (clay on his eyes)
5. How many friends did the paralyzed man have? (four)
6. What member of Peter's family had a fever? (mother-in-law)
7. What does Ephphatha mean? (be opened)
8. What troubled the woman who had a spirit of infirmity for eighteen years? (a crooked back)
9. What day of the week did Jesus heal the man with a withered hand? (Sabbath)
10. Did Jesus heal the nobleman's son in Capernaum by touch? (no)
11. What does it mean to be deaf and dumb? (unable to hear and speak)
12. Who is the Great Physician? (Jesus)

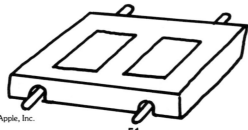

SS845

# TEACHING HELPS
## CORNSTARCH CLAY

If you have limited resources, you may use this simple recipe for clay.

1 cup salt
½ cup cornstarch
½ cup boiling water
food coloring

Stir all ingredients together over low heat until smooth. Store in sealed container.

## CUTOUT LETTERS

Letters are always needed for posters or bulletin boards. They may be cut from art paper, magazines, wallpaper, etc.

Cut out squares the size you wish letters to be. Draw a capital "I" to use as a guide in drawing and cutting the rest of letters of the alphabet. In this way, the height and width of all letters can be kept consistent. A small piece of sandpaper attached to the back of a letter will make it stick on a flannel board.

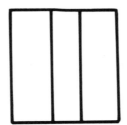  

## FILE AWAY

There are many items that can be saved for future use. If a file cabinet is not available, a heavy cardboard box is fine; and make your own subject dividers. Items to file include teaching pictures, Bible scenes, magazine pictures, plastic-covered puzzles, games, maps, etc.

At an office supply ask for the box that poster board was shipped in. Use it to file poster board games and activities.

Shoe boxes may be used to file 3″ x 5″ cards containing questions and answers, matching games, memory verses, etc. File by subject.

Always be on the alert for ideas to help in your teaching efforts. Be an accumulator; keep a filing system to store away those ideas or activities. Be orderly and you will never have to turn your home or classroom upside down looking for a particular picture or activity!

SS845

# MAKER OF MIRACLES

The four Gospels describe thirty-five occasions when Jesus performed miracles. These include those times when He healed the sick and raised the dead, and also when He showed His mighty power over things: feeding a large crowd with a boy's small lunch, walking on water, stilling a storm, changing water into wine and catching huge numbers of fish. Then there was His own glorious Resurrection, the miracle of miracles!

SS845

# MIRACLES OF JESUS

This puzzle tells about seven of Jesus' miracles. Use either the clues on the left or unscramble the scrambled answers on the right.

CLUES

1. Told to be still
2. A tree that was withered
3. An overflowing fish net
4. Jesus walked upon it
5. In a fish's mouth
6. It fed a multitude
7. Water at a wedding

M
I
R
A
C
L
E

1. **M** O R S T
2. **I** F G
3. **R** B E K O
4. **A** E R T W
5. **C** I N O
6. **L** C H N U
7. **E** I N W

SS845

# MUSIC! MUSIC! MUSIC!

A wedding celebration in biblical times often lasted from one to two weeks! When Jesus attended the wedding in Cana, He heard music and singing. Music has always been an expression of joy and praise. The children may use the simple instruments below as part of a puppet show, a choral reading or for the pure fun of it!

## POTPIE PERCUSSION

Save potpie tins and give two to each pupil. Instruct them to punch two holes in one, as shown. A nail can serve as a hole puncher. Insert a 6" inch length of yarn or string through the holes, forming a loop. Knot the ends inside the tin. Have children pour ¼ cup of dried beans into the second tin. Place the other on top and staple the two tins securely together. You have just made a shaker!

Give each pupil another pie tin and six to ten bottle caps with holes punched in them. Punch holes evenly around the edge of the tin. Direct children to cut short pieces of yarn or string and use them to attach the caps to the tin. The tambourine is now ready to rattle!

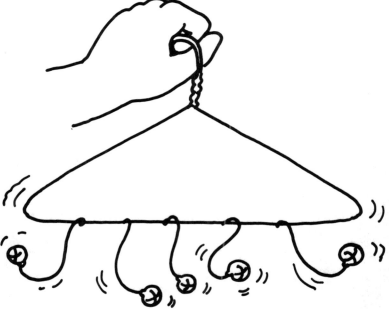

## COAT HANGER JINGLE

Give each pupil a coat hanger. It may be wrapped with yarn for color. Purchase small bells at a craft store. Using either yarn or ribbon, have the children attach the bells to the hangers. Different-sized bells may be used to give different sounds. The children are ready to jingle and jangle!

# PETER WALKS UPON THE WATER

## Choral Reading
### by
### Lucille Golphenee

To present this poem, set up a scene using classroom furnishings. On the left place a table to serve as a mountain. On the right, place two rows containing twelve chairs to represent the Disciples' boat. You may play a recording of storm sounds, or enlist some children to provide sound effects during the reading.

Have two children read the quotes of Jesus and Peter as they appear. Those playing Jesus and the Disciples should also perform the actions of the story. Encourage pupils to put emotion into their readings and to give life to the story being told.

### I

Jesus went up on the mountain
By Himself, apart, to pray.
After He had healed the sick ones,
And had sent them on their way,
The Disciples went before Him,
Took a ship, and set to sea;
But a storm came up about them,
And the waves tossed angrily.

### II

Then the Master came to join them,
In the fourth watch of the night.
He came walking on the waters,
And the men shrank back in fright;
They thought they had seen a spirit,
And they all cried out in fear;
But the Lord spoke comfort, saying,
"It is I; be of good cheer."

### III

Then did Peter answer Jesus,
"Lord, if it is really You,
Just say the word, and I'll come
Walking on the water, too."
Then the Master's voice was tender
As he said so gently, "Come."
Peter started out to meet Him,
Looking to the Holy One.

### IV

But his heart began to fail him
When he of the storm did think;
Then he saw the angry waters,
And his feet began to sink.
Now the man was terror-stricken,
And feared that he should die.
As he looked up to the Master,
"Save me, Lord!" was Peter's cry.

### V

Jesus then reached forth in mercy,
And he quickly pulled him out,
But His loving heart was saddened
As he said, "Why did you doubt?"

### VI

When they came into the vessel,
Then the boistrous winds did cease.
Stormy seas obey His bidding
When the Master whispers, "Peace."
Then all were filled with praises
For the mighty works He'd done,
And they worshipped Jesus, saying,
"It is true, You are God's Son."

SS845

# WATER, WATER EVERYWHERE

Many of Jesus' miracles occurred in or around water. Here are two activities related to water. As the pupils participate in them you may talk about the water miracles. Locate the Sea of Galilee on a map, perhaps wondering with the children what it would be like to be a fisherman in biblical times.

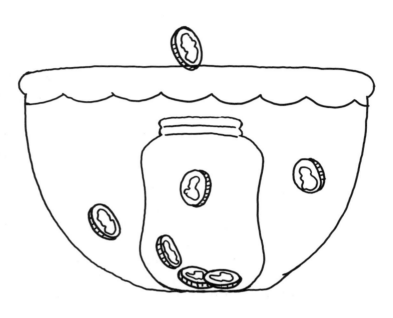

This is a simple game that requires a large bowl of water with a small empty coffee jar submerged in the center. The children take turns dropping pennies into the bowl, trying to get the coins to land inside the coffee jar. Before passing out the pennies, tell the story of the fish with the coin in its mouth (Matthew 17:24-27).

There is another world under the surface of a lake, river or creek. The children will enjoy using a "water scope" to get a glimpse of that world.

MATERIALS:
A half-gallon paper milk carton, a sheet of clear plastic or a plastic bag, and four rubber bands.

PROCEDURE:
Have pupils cut off the top and bottom of milk carton. (Help, if necessary.) Put the plastic over one end and secure with the rubber bands.

Instruct the children to use their water-scope only when a grown-up is with them. They can lie down at the water's edge and put the plastic covered end into the water while they look through the other end. The scope does not need to be submerged very deep. Ask the pupils to make a list of all they see in God's underwater world.

SS845

# POSE A MIRACLE

Encourage pupils to do most of the planning for this activity. Their enthusiastic participation will create a rich learning experience.

## MATERIALS:
Simple costumes, props, a 35 mm camera, roll of slide film, a projector and a tape recorder.

## PROCEDURE:
The pupils must first decide what miracles they want to present: changing water to wine, coin in fish's mouth, walking on the water, etc. Assign three or four pupils to a miracle. Give those groups the responsibility of determining how the scene should be staged, who will be in it, where it can be performed and what props will be needed. Suggest that the same pupil portray Jesus in every miracle.

## COSTUMES AND PROPS:
A striped, or solid-colored fabric 36" square will make a suitable head covering. Fasten in place with a cloth strip tied around the head or with a stretchy headband. Simple costumes can be constructed by measuring a 45" width of cloth twice the height of the child. Fold in half lengthwise and cut a pattern as shown. Stitch sides and underarms. Garment may be tied at the waist with a rope or necktie. Props should be kept simple. Many can be made with heavyweight paper: fish, clay jars, clouds, even a boat. Let the children use their rich imaginations for creating props.

## POSING SCENES:
Scenes may be posed outdoors. If you have a lake or other body of water nearby, the water miracles can be shot there. If everything is to be done in or around the church, select places that will add realism to the scene. A large piece of blue fabric can represent a sea. When shooting the scenes be sure to take at least two shots of each, one to serve as a back-up. Again, allow the pupils to be creative in developing their own ideas.

## PRESENTATION:
While waiting for the film to be developed, the pupils can begin writing a narrative. This can be refined when they see the pictures for the first time. The narrative may be taped and played as the slides are being shown, or the narration can be read. Older children will enjoy giving the slide presentation to younger groups. Store the slides and tape for future use.

Any area of Jesus' life may be portrayed in this way.

SS845

# FEEDING THE MULTITUDE

The story of the feeding of the five thousand can be found in all four Gospels: Matthew 14:15-21, Mark 6:35-44, Luke 9:12-17 and John 6:5-14. Share the story with the children. The following game and activity will help the pupils to thank God for their food, while testing their knowledge of the miracle of the feeding of the five thousand.

## THANK YOU, GOD

You will need paper place mats, paper plates, small paper cups, napkins and plastic utensils. Pass out a place setting to each pupil and direct them to glue the pieces on the mat, as shown. In the center of the plate have them print THANK YOU, GOD. Hang poster on refrigerator or near the dining room table at home.

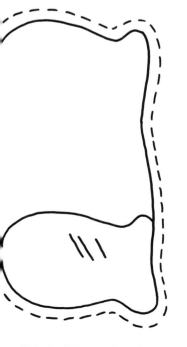

## LOAVES AND FISHES

On a poster board glue a construction paper basket. Leave the top open for inserting two fishes and five loaves made from the patterns provided here. On each of the fishes and loaves, print a question about the feeding of the five thousand. If you like, seven more questions can be included on the reverse sides. Instruct the pupils to select a loaf or a fish and answer the question. After the game is completed, you may serve the class pieces of pita or Arabic bread and tuna fish, or fish-shaped crackers. Be sure to give thanks for the food.

SS845

# WALKING ON WATER

Share John 6:16-21, which records the miracle of Jesus walking on water. Reproduce the boat scene and the figure of Jesus found on page 61. Each pupil will need six copies. They may be colored after the project is completed. Instruct the class to cut out the boat scenes and the six figures of Jesus. Glue the six figures of Jesus, one to each page, so that He is drawing closer to the boat in each scene. Staple the pages together on the left side of the booklet, and flip the pages rapidly to make Jesus "walk" on water toward the boat.

# STILLING THE STORM

Read Mark 4:35-41, which describes Jesus calming the storm. Give each pupil a large piece of paper with a line drawn down the middle. Instruct the class to create two pictures—one that shows the stormy sea and one that shows the sea after Jesus commanded it to be still. Pupils may use the patterns on the next page in composing their pictures. Encourage children with artistic talent to draw their own scenes.

Shining Star Publications, Copyright © 1988, A division of Good Apple, Inc.

SS845

# WALKING ON WATER PATTERNS

SS845

# THE FABULOUS FISH CATCH

There are two accounts of Jesus miraculously providing the Disciples with a huge catch of fish. The first occurs early in His ministry and is related in Luke 5:1-9, the second occurs after His Resurrection (John 21:1-11). Share both accounts with the children. Use the following game to reinforce information on the life of Jesus. Make the answers numbers: how many wise men, Disciples, days in tomb, number of people fed, days in the wilderness, etc.

You will need a fisherman's dip net; or make a net, using nylon netting and a bent coat hanger. Cut out fish using pattern found below. Glue two cut-out fish together around the edges leaving the mouth open. Print questions on pieces of paper. Roll up and insert in fishes' mouth.

Pass the net among the children, and have each child withdraw a fish from the net. They should take the question from the fish's mouth and attempt to answer it correctly. If they answer correctly, they keep the fish. If they answer incorrectly, they must put the question back in the fish and return it to the net. Continue until all the fish are "caught."

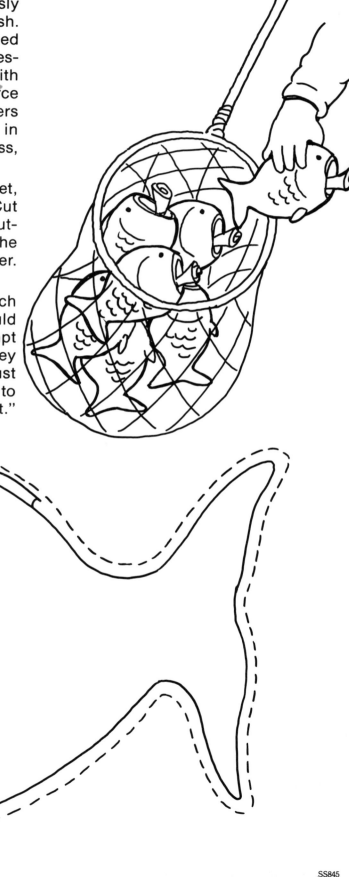

62

# HANG THEM OUT TO DRY

Use the pattern to make several of these robes in different colors.

Hang a heavy string or rope from wall to wall. The children may write a Bible verse on each robe, or they may want to draw pictures on them, or write the names of the Disciples. Discuss how the robes will be used, and then provide markers, crayons and any other needed materials.

When the pupils are done, hang the robes on the line with clothespins. Explain that when the Disciples were caught in that terrible storm, their clothes were soaked. We are hanging the robes out to dry!

Shining Star Publications, Copyright © 1988, A division of Good Apple, Inc.

SS845

# SEASONAL ACTIVITIES

## A HEARTFELT MESSAGE

Children will enjoy giving these bookmarks to family and friends. You will need 1″ wide white ribbon and red construction paper. Cut out six 2″ hearts for each pupil. Direct them to glue the hearts back-to-back over the ribbon. They should then print on one side "JESUS LOVES YOU," and on the reverse side "SO DO I." Or they may use "GOD LOVES YOU" and "JESUS PROVES IT."

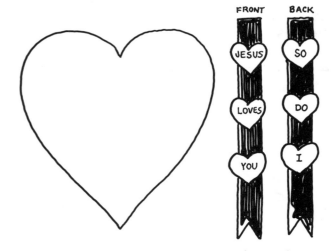

## GIFT FOR MOTHER

The pupils will be pleased to give their mothers these unusual soap Bibles. You will need white felt, narrow red ribbon, gold soap bars and Jesus stickers. Cut felt into 4″ x 6″ pieces and round off corners. Cut ribbon into 6″ lengths, forming bookmarks. Tell children to glue ribbon lengthwise to the left side of the bar with an inch extending at each end.

Then have the children fold the felt in half and glue it around the soap so that all the edges are even. Place a sticker on the front. Older children can write "BIBLE" on the front, using markers or stick-on letters.

## WORDS FROM JESUS

In Luke 18:1 Jesus says ". . . men ought always to pray . . . ." These words will make a meaningful gift for children to give their fathers on Father's Day. You will need 4″ x 5″ pieces of construction paper, with holes and slits placed as shown. Yarn may be used as a hanger. Cut out the inserts from white paper, using the measurements indicated. Print the verse on the inserts and then have children fasten them into the frames. They may decorate the wall hangings with glitter, yarn, stickers or their own drawings.

# PARABLES WITH PEOPLE

Jesus often taught by telling parables—stories that contain a lesson. Many of these are parables about people from all walks of life: a rich fool; an unjust judge; a faithful shepherd; a good neighbor; a wasteful son. All of these parables help the listener to better understand God and the kingdom of heaven. They also challenge us to live better lives. The people in them will be remembered forever!

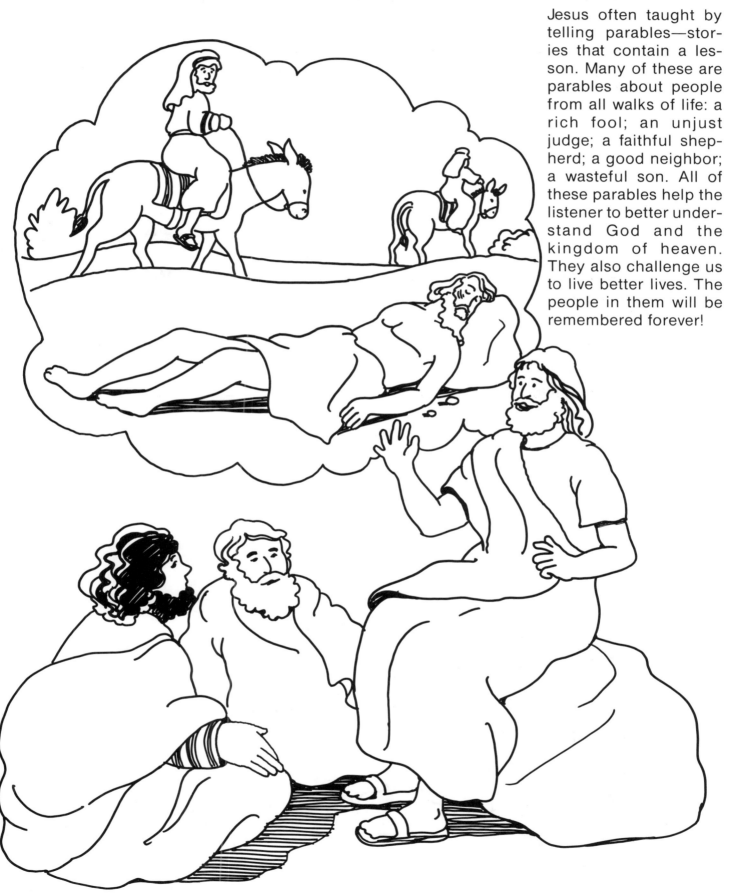

SS845

# WHO ARE THESE PEOPLE?

Fill in these spaces with people in Jesus' stories. Use the clues and if you need more help, use the Scripture references. Next move the letters from the squares to the numbered squares below and learn the special name for these stories.

1. Son who wandered   ☐ __ __ __ __ __ __   Luke 15:11-32
2. The good neighbor   __ ☐ __ __ __ __ __ __ __   Luke 10:33
3. There were ten   __ __ ☐ __ __ __ __ __   Matthew 25:1
4. Found in vineyard   __ ☐ __ __ __ __ __ __ __   Matthew 20:1
5. They owed money   __ __ ☐ __ __ __ __   Luke 7:41
6. He was rich   __ __ __ ☐   Luke 12:19,20
7. He was unfair   __ __ ☐ __ __ __ __   Luke 16:1
8. The bragging prayer   __ __ __ __ __ ☐ __ __   Luke 18:11

☐ ☐ ☐ ☐ ☐ ☐ ☐ ☐
1   2   3   4   5   6   7   8

SS845

# THE GOOD SAMARITAN
## Choral Reading
## by Lucille Golphenee

Luke 10:25-37 is the parable of the Good Samaritan. This reading may be presented as a simple pantomime. Select pupils to be robbers, the injured man, the priest, the Levite, the Samaritan and the innkeeper. Draw faces on paper plates and attach to tongue depressors. Yarn and cloth may be added for facial features. The pupils are to hold the plates in front of their faces as they act out the story. Two groups may alternately read the poem. Within the groups pupils may like to use a single reader, or alternate voices. Encourage creative thinking. A Scripture reader will begin and end the parable.

**SCRIPTURE READER:** Luke 10:25-29

**ALL:** The Master answered a certain lawyer, by telling him this story:

**GROUP A:**
A man went from Jerusalem
   To Jericho one day.
Some thieves came and attacked him,
   As he journeyed on his way.
They took from him his clothing,
   And they struck him 'til he bled,
Then turned and went the other way
   And left him there for dead.

**GROUP B:**
By chance there came a certain priest
   And saw him lying there;
He crossed the street and passed him up,
   As if he didn't care.
Then came a Levite, walking by,
   And when he reached the spot,
He hurried on his busy way,
   And very soon forgot.

**GROUP A:**
At last came a Samaritan
   And looked upon the man;
His heart was saddened as he said,
   "I'll help him if I can."
He fixed his wounds, and bound them up,
   And poured in oil and wine;
And then he took him to an inn,
   And cared for him just fine.

**GROUP B:**
The next day, then, he paid the host,
   And said, "I have to go.
Please do your best to care for him,
   And gentle kindness show.
Whatever more you have to spend,
   Be it three pence or ten,
I surely will repay you all
   When I come back again."

**SCRIPTURE READER:** Luke 10:36-37

**ALL:**
A neighbor, then, is one who cares,
   And shows it by his actions.

SS845

# GOOD SHEPHERD GAME

To make the spinner for this game, you will need a small paper plate and a brad to hold the cardboard arrow in place. Glue numbered circle to center of plate and attach the arrow. Reproduce gameboard on page 69, glue to cardboard and cover with clear Con-Tact paper. Children may use different colored buttons as markers. They are to take turns spinning the arrow and moving their marker the number of spaces indicated. The object is to be the first to reach the lost sheep.

SS845

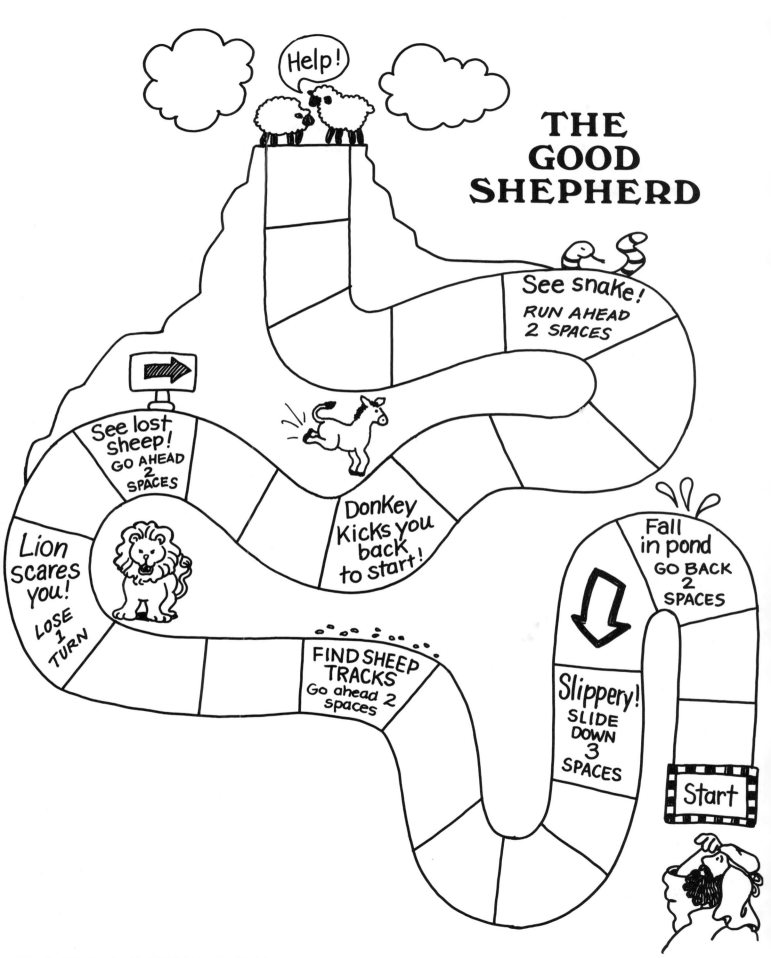

SS845

# THE PRODIGAL SON

The parable of the Prodigal Son is found in Luke 15:11-32.

To depict this story, color the figures on this page and page 71. Cut out figures and glue a small piece of sandpaper to the back of each. A lightweight board covered with blue flannel can be used as a background. Clouds and grass can be cut out and backed with sandpaper or may be drawn on the flannel with colored chalk. As you tell the story, display the appropriate figures, as indicated.

Jesus told the story of a man (father) who had two sons. The younger one (son) came to his father and asked for his inheritance so that he could see the world. The father reluctantly gave the money to his son. (Place money bag in father's hand and then move to son's.) The boy left feeling very happy. (Remove father.) Time passed and the son made some terrible mistakes. He lost all his money (Remove bag.) and had no place to stay or any food to eat. A man offered him a job taking care of his pigs. (Place pigs and boy in ragged clothes.) It was not pleasant work for a young man used to having everything he ever wanted. He was always hungry and even ate the same food as the pigs. He finally could take no more and decided to go back home. He would ask his father to forgive him and beg him to take him back as one of the servants. (Remove figures and place mountain scene and boy with stick.) The boy made the long trip home with a heavy heart. He felt his father would be too ashamed of him to take him back. Just then the father looked out a window and saw the ragged boy approaching his house. He knew in a moment who it was and rushed out to greet him. (Place Father with open arms.) He called the servants and told them to bring a ring for the boy's finger and a robe to place over his tattered clothes. (Remove walking son and place robed son.) He also commanded the servants to prepare a great banquet. He declared that his son who was lost was now found. It was a time of great joy!

SS845

# THE PRODIGAL SON PATTERNS

SS845

# THE PRODIGAL SON RETURNS MAZE

Can you find the road that will take the Prodigal Son home again?

72

SS845

# FUN WITH DIORAMAS

Children enjoy making dioramas. A diorama is a little scene in a box. It is viewed through an open side of the box. The pupils may create very simple or very eaborate dioramas. Provide shoe boxes, clay, pipe cleaners, crayons, paints, scissors and any other odds and ends to represent objects and figures.

Assign two or three children to work on a scene that depicts one of the parables about people. Decide what kind of background to make. The background can be drawn on paper and then glued to the back and sides of the box. Trees, clouds, etc. can be cut out and glued to the paper. Small branches stuck in clay make realistic trees. A piece of a green terry cloth towel can serve as grass. A small pocket mirror can become a lake, and blue ribbons can become rivers. Figures can be made with pipe cleaners, supported by clay, or they can be shaped of clay. Pictures of Bible people, animals or objects may be cut out of magazines and then glued to sticks and put in clay. Let the pupils try various ideas. You will be surprised at their ingenuity!

Shining Star Publications, Copyright © 1988, A division of Good Apple, Inc.

SS845

# A CHORAL PLAY

Throughout the book you will find choral readings based on different parts of Jesus' life. There are suggested presentations for each; but you are encouraged to use your own or your students' creative ideas.

These six readings may be used as scenes of a choral play depicting the life of Jesus.

Soft music may be played in the background or appropriate songs sung that depict certain times in Jesus' life. The song "The Lord's Prayer" is found on page 89. Other original songs are on pages 23, 47, and 136. Simple props and costumes may be used. The introductory paragraphs of each chapter can be read by a narrator. The introductions connect the readings and allow the play to flow smoothly.

The children may present the play in the church sanctuary, in classrooms or even in nursing homes or homes of shut-ins. The play should be adapted to different situations.

SS845

# PARABLES WITH OBJECTS

The parables of Jesus not only included people from different walks of life, they were also based on everyday things. His listeners were often farmers who could relate to stories of planting, harvest, seeds, tares, sheep or goats. Women were familiar with leaven, patching old cloth, or the despair of losing a silver coin. These simple stories enabled Jesus to teach difficult concepts about God's love and His mighty Kingdom.

SS845

# OBJECTIVELY SPEAKING

Use the picture clues to fill in the puzzle. If you need help, use the Scripture references to find the objects in Jesus' parables.

ACROSS

1. Pesky

Matthew 13:25

3. Mustard

Mark 4:31

4. Rising

Luke 13:21

DOWN

1. Hidden

Matthew 13:44

2. Precious

Matthew 13:46

5. Lost

Luke 15:8 (NIV)

SS845

# PARABLE OF THE SEEDS

OBJECTIVE: To help the pupils understand the lesson of the parable of the seeds as found in Matthew 13:3-8

MATERIALS: Cover board with blue paper. On strip of paper cut out or print "SOWING SEEDS." Place top center. Enlarge sower with an overhead projector and attach to the left side of the board. Use large seeds, such as almonds or lima beans, and glue them as if they were falling from sower's hand. Cut out four large seed shapes of the same size. On the first shape, glue seeds on brown paper (soil) and have birds eating them. On the second shape, place a large yellow sun. Wheat stalks may be made from heavy beige or yellow yarn or paper. Cut out grey stones and glue around the wilted wheat on light green background. On the third seed pattern, glue the yarn wheat on green background, and intertwine with dark green yarn to represent a thorny bush. Short pieces of yarn knotted at intervals will make thorns. On the last seed, glue a mass of wheat standing tall on a dark green background.

PROCEDURE: Share the parable of the seeds from Matthew. Ask the children to point to the seeds on the bulletin board as they are mentioned in the story. Next, read Matthew 13:18-23 which is Jesus' interpretation of the parable as told to the Disciples. Call on pupils to explain the meaning of each seed. Before class, prepare seed-shaped cards. Print or type short descriptions of people who are representatives of the four seeds: a person who refuses a Bible; a man who attends church regularly for awhile and then never returns; a girl who lives by God's Word until she makes new friends who are not Christians; and a woman who is known for her kindness, loving heart and deep faith. Provide two or three examples for each seed. Pass out cards to the pupils, and as they are read aloud, have the children tell which seed on the board fits their story. Lead a discussion on how the person in each story might be led to be more fruitful for Jesus.

# A PICTURE PROJECTOR

You may make three or four projectors for your class use, or have each student make his own. In either case you will need paper towel tubes, two Popsicle sticks for each tube and white paper.

To make the viewer, cut a 2" piece from the end of tube. Lay the pieces down as shown with a little space between them. Take one Popsicle stick and glue so that it holds the two pieces together. Glue the other stick next to it. Don't forget the space!

To make the filmstrips, reproduce the patterns provided. If the pupils make individual viewers, give each child a copy of the strips. Instruct the children to put the strip in the slot and hold the tube up to a light. As they pull the paper along they will be able to see the parable objects. Ask them to identify each object and tell which parable it represents.

If the pupils would like to make their own strips, provide 2" x 8" long strips of white paper divided into 4 equal squares. They may then use dark crayons or markers to draw scenes or objects.

Any area of Jesus' life can be described with appropriate strips.

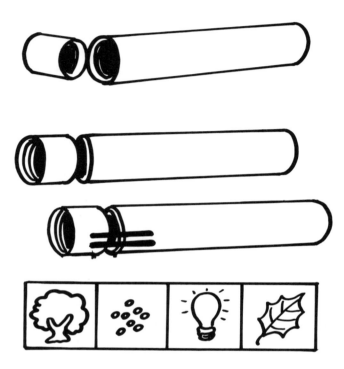

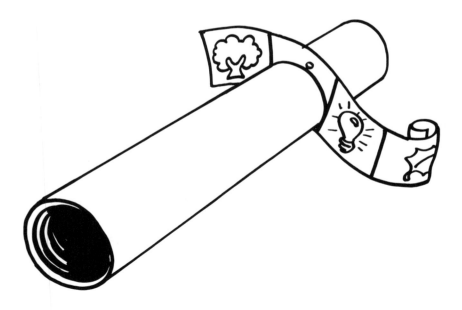

# PICTURE PROJECTOR STRIPS

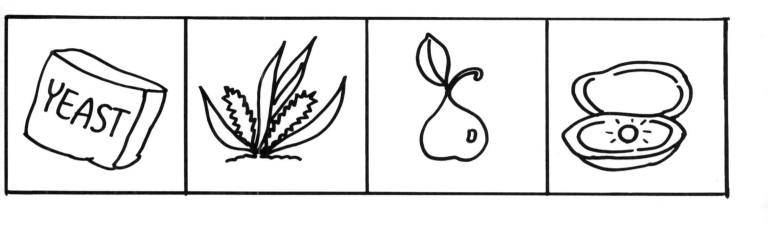

SS845

# FOOD FOR FUN

## PASS THE SALT!

Foods are mentioned in some parables. Share Matthew 5:13. Conduct a taste test using both salted and unsalted nuts. You can blindfold the tasters for a real test of their taste buds. Ask what differences they observe in the two nuts. Have a pupil find the definition of "savor" and read it to the class. Discuss what it means to be the salt of the earth. Share with children that before refrigeration Bible people used salt to preserve their foods, and it was very precious.

## THE FABULOUS FIG!

Read Mark 13:28. For a treat have dried figs or cookies with a fig center. Jesus often used the fig in His parables. Tell the children a few things about figs. The summer fig of Bible lands is sweet and purple in color. Long ago, cakes made of figs were used to cover sores and cuts. The sycamore fig is one of the largest trees in Palestine and is sometimes fifty feet around. It is almost the only tree that grows in Egypt, and every part is used. To sit under the shade of your own fig tree was considered to be the fullest kind of peace.

## LET IT RISE!

Read Matthew 13:33. Mention that in Bible times women kept back a portion of old dough and added it to a new batch to make it rise. The resulting bread had a sour taste and smell. Bakers today use yeast to make the bread we enjoy. The leaven in Jesus' parable is used to illustrate the growth of the kingdom of heaven.

Arrange to bake bread in the church kitchen or at home. A box of hot roll mix or frozen bread dough can be used. You will want the children to see the effect of the yeast as it doubles the size of the dough. If possible, serve the bread hot, with butter and fig preserves—a snack children of Bible times might have relished!

SS845

# SPELLING WITH FIGS

On poster board draw a large tree, or cut one from green and brown paper and glue to the poster. Cut out figs from purple paper and print the letters from the following words on them: coin, tares, seed, salt, fig, pearl, etc. Place a small loop of tape on the back of each fig and scatter around the tree, using straight pins to fasten them in place. Give clues for the objects and call on pupils to come up and select the figs that spell the object you are describing. Pin the correctly spelled words on the bulletin board background.

SS845

# THE LOST COIN GAME

This is a simple game to be used while teaching the parable of the lost coin, found in Luke 15:8-10. Cut several saucer-sized circles from grey paper and print "$1" on each. Before the children arrive, hide the "coins" around the room.

If you have a silver dollar, use it as a visual aid. Tell the children that silver dollars today are worth more than a paper dollar because silver is more valuable. Some are worth ten dollars or more! If you lost a silver dollar, you would certainly search for it, just as the woman did in Jesus' parable. Share the details of the story. At the conclusion instruct the pupils to search the room for the "lost coins." You may wish to print questions about the lesson on the backs of the coins.

You may purchase nickel coin holders from a department store and insert a coin in each. On the holders print "The Lost Coin, Luke 15:8-10" and give one to each child to take home.

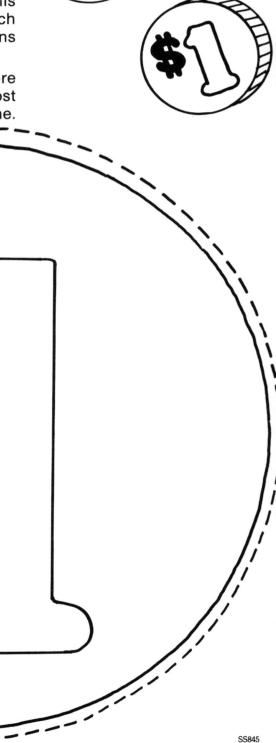

# MATCH THE OBJECT

On a piece of poster board, or a bulletin board attach strips of paper containing the Scripture references shown here. Each reference refers to a parable. On a display table placed directly beneath the poster, place the following objects: a packet of seeds; a paper cup filled with weeds; a pearl necklace; a salt shaker; a packet of yeast; one coin. Have the students look up each verse and then use a long piece of yarn (already glued to each paper strip) to connect the verse with its matching object on the table. Use a paper clip to attach the yarn or tie the yarn to the object. You may need to create a loop or other fastener on the object ahead of time, so that the children can attach the yarn.

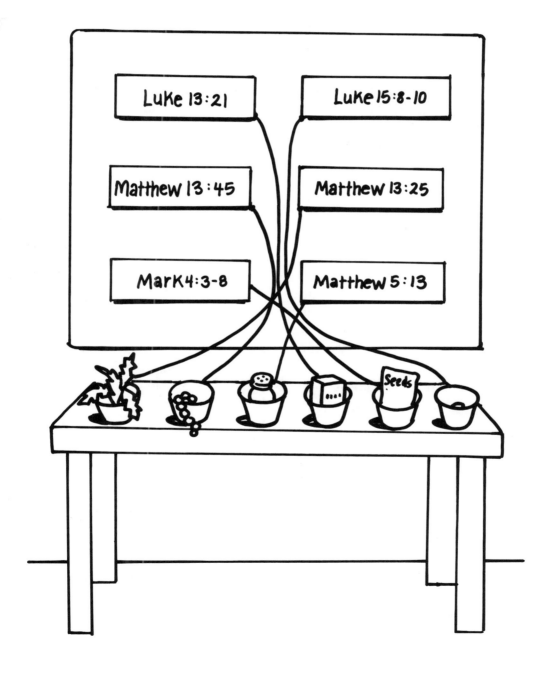

SS845

# THE ART OF STORYTELLING

Some teachers find it difficult to tell a story. They instead read it word for word with little expression or enthusiasm. The parables of Jesus are the highest form of storytelling. Any teacher can benefit from following their example.

1. Use terms and expressions your age group will understand, as Jesus did.

2. The parables are short. Choose your words carefully and don't get carried away with adjectives and side issues.

3. Can you imagine Jesus telling His parables without expression? Throw yourself into the story. Smile, moan, frown, exclaim, enjoy! The children will respond to your enthusiasm.

4. Know your story and do a little research and learn even more.

5. Some teachers find they are more comfortable if they have something to hold: a teaching picture, an object related to the story, a flannelgraph, a puppet, etc. Try different methods and see what will help you break out of the "head down, reading word for word" method. All your efforts will be appreciated by the children who will be hanging on to your every word!

# A PAPER THEATER

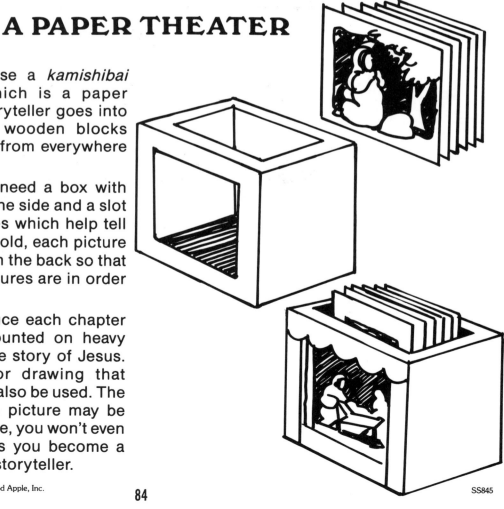

In Japan, storytellers use a *kamishibai* (kah-mee-shee-by), which is a paper theater in a box. The storyteller goes into a park and claps two wooden blocks together. Children come from everywhere to see and hear his story.

For the theater you will need a box with a framed opening cut in the side and a slot in the top to hold pictures which help tell the story. As the story is told, each picture is pulled out and placed in the back so that at the conclusion the pictures are in order for the next telling.

The pictures that introduce each chapter in this book can be mounted on heavy paper and used to tell the story of Jesus. Any teaching picture or drawing that depicts a Bible story may also be used. The words telling about each picture may be printed on the back. In time, you won't even need to refer to them, as you become a more relaxed and happy storyteller.

SS845

# WHEN JESUS PRAYED

Jesus set the example for a meaningful prayer life. He prayed both morning and evening, and in Luke 6:12 it is recorded that He even prayed all night long. Jesus' own personal need for prayer was vividly demonstrated in the Garden of Gethsemane. The Lord's Prayer from the Sermon on the Mount is a beautiful prayer for every believer.

SS845

# THE PRAYERS OF JESUS

These ten sentences tell when and where Jesus prayed. Complete each sentence with the correct word. If you need help, look up the Scriptures below.

1. Jesus prayed as He was being __ __ **P** __ __ __ __ __ by John.

2. He rose early in the __ __ **R** __ __ __ __ to pray.

3. He prayed in __ __ __ __ __ __ __ **A** __ __ as the Disciples slept.

4. On the cross of __ __ __ __ __ __ **Y** He prayed for His enemies.

5. He went out late in the __ __ **E** __ __ __ __ to pray alone.

6. He withdrew to the __ __ __ __ __ **R** __ __ __ to pray.

7. He gave **T** __ __ __ __ __ for a boy's lunch.

8. Jesus placed His hands on the __ __ **I** __ __ __ __ __ and prayed.

9. He went up a **M** __ __ __ __ __ __ __ to pray.

10. He prayed at a last __ __ __ __ **E** __ with His Disciples.

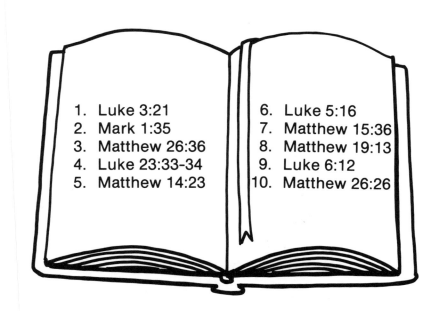

| | |
|---|---|
| 1. Luke 3:21 | 6. Luke 5:16 |
| 2. Mark 1:35 | 7. Matthew 15:36 |
| 3. Matthew 26:36 | 8. Matthew 19:13 |
| 4. Luke 23:33-34 | 9. Luke 6:12 |
| 5. Matthew 14:23 | 10. Matthew 26:26 |

SS845

# A TIME TO PRAY

OBJECTIVE: This bulletin board provides an opportunity for children to actively participate in prayer. Their prayers may come from their own personal needs, but they should be encouraged to remember others as well.

MATERIALS: You will need colored paper to serve as background on the whole board. Use a piece of flannel in a contrasting color, and measuring 24" x 24," to place in the center of the board. Use a 1" paper to form border around outside edges. Enlarge the figure of the praying child and add it to the display. Cut out the large letters, or print them on a strip of paper. Make two pockets, using 3" x 5" cards. One should be labeled "PRAY" and the other "TODAY." Attach to the board below the flannel square.

PROCEDURE: Instruct children to write their prayers on blank 3" x 5" cards which have had sandpaper pieces glued to the back. Place cards in the "PRAY" pocket. When prayer time comes, seat the children in front of the board, and pull out the cards. Ask children to write their requests on the cards, and then attach cards to the flannel. Call on different children to pray, reminding them to limit the length of their prayer. At the conclusion of prayer time, have the children write more requests and place them in the "TODAY" pocket. At the end of the day, pass out the cards to the students to use at home during their private prayers.

SS845

# A PRAYER FROM JESUS

Jesus taught the Lord's Prayer on two occasions. In Luke 11:1-4 He was asked by the Disciples to teach them to pray. The familiar version of the Lord's Prayer is found in the Sermon on the Mount, Matthew 6:9-13.

## MEMORIZING

Encourage the children to memorize this special prayer from Jesus. Consider making the Lord's Prayer a regular part of your class time. To promote memorization, hang a brightly colored 1" wide ribbon on the wall or bulletin board. When a child memorizes the prayer, print his name on a copy of the seal shown here and pin or glue it to the ribbon. Use the song on the following page to teach the words of the Lord's Prayer to the children.

## A PICTURE OF PRAYER

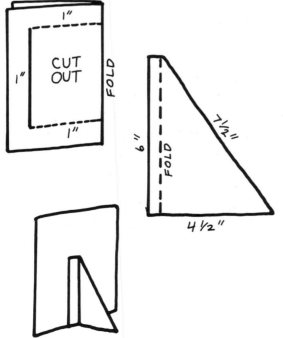

Cut a piece of lightweight cardboard 7" x 9" to serve as backing. Fold a piece of 7" x 9" construction paper in half and lengthwise and cut out the center portion, creating a 1" frame, as shown. Give each child a copy of the song "The Lord's Prayer," that appears on the next page. Cut to fit, and glue the prayer song to the cardboard. Next, glue the paper frame over the prayer. Make a triangular back support as illustrated and glue to the back of the frame. The children will enjoy decorating the frame with stickers, stars, yarn, glitter, etc.

SS845

# THE LORD'S PRAYER

## Music by Helen Friesen

Text from Matt. 6:9-13

SS845

# A PRAYER PLACE

In Matthew 6:6 Jesus taught, "But thou, when thou prayest, enter into thy closet, and when thou hast shut thy door, pray to thy Father which is in secret; and thy Father which seeth in secret shall reward thee openly."

In most classrooms, because of the many planned activities, a child has very little opportunity for quiet time with God. A "Prayer Place" set up in a corner of the room will give the children a chance to enter a "closet" and pray in secret with their Father for a few minutes each day.

MATERIALS: To create a prayer place, you will need a large cardboard box obtained from a furniture or appliance store. Set the box up in a corner of the classroom. Cut a door large enough for a child to enter. Let the children decorate the box. They might like to draw or paint flowers on the outside. They could also use the wall hanging or prayer reminders found in this chapter, as decorations. Inside place a chair and a small table (or a box turned upside down). Set another table outside the door. On it place a stand-up sign which says "OPEN" on one side and "PRAYING" on the reverse. Also include two egg-timers, one on the outside table and one inside.

PROCEDURE: Discuss with the children the need to spend time alone talking to God or just being quiet in His presence. Read Matthew 6:6. Ask why Jesus thought it was better to talk to God in secret. Remind the class of those who prayed in public just to be seen by others. Instruct the children that the prayer place can only be used by one child at a time. They can enter whenever they have finished with their work or during activity time. When a child enters the enclosure, he should make sure the sign is turned to "PRAYING." He sets both timers so that he (and those outside) knows when his quiet time is up. As the child leaves the prayer place he turns the sign back over to read "OPEN."

SS845

# A WALL HANGING

The Bible teaches that Jesus prayed morning and evening. This wall hanging will serve to remind children that they may talk to God any time of the day.

Materials: A 10" dowel, yarn and an 8" x 16" piece of felt, burlap or other heavy cloth. Instruct the children to glue the top over the dowel and attach the yarn to form a hanger. The bottom of the fabric may be hemmed. Instruct students to use the patterns to cut out two suns, two mountains and the letters "P-r-a-y." They may use fabric or heavy paper. The children will then glue the pieces in place as illustrated.

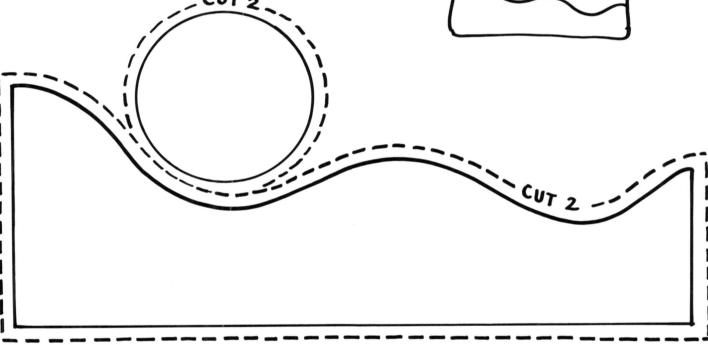

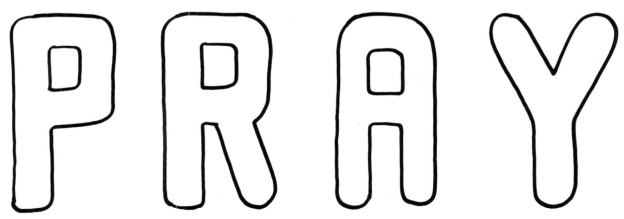

# PRAYERS ON PAPER

1. Write the Lord's Prayer in your own words. If you are unsure of the meaning of some words, look them up in a dictionary.

2. Write three short prayers asking God's help for
   a. a sick friend
   b. a missionary
   c. an elderly person

3. Make a list of those things for which you are grateful to God. Write a short prayer of thanks.

Shining Star Publications, Copyright © 1988, A division of Good Apple, Inc.

SS845

# FRAMED VERSES AND MOTTOES

Give each child a 4″ x 5″ piece of construction paper with two holes in the top center and two vertical slits 2″ in length, as shown. String or yarn may be used as a hanger. Cut out the inserts from white paper, using the dimensions listed here. Print or type a motto or verse about prayer on it. (Some of the suggested verses are excerpts.) The children are to insert the white paper into the frame and then decorate the hanging with yarn, glitter, seals, etc.

SUGGESTED VERSES:    "Watch and pray." (Matthew 26:41)
                     "Pray always." (Luke 21:36)
                     "Pray without ceasing." (I Thessalonians 5:17)
                     "Lord, teach us to pray." (Luke 11:1)

SUGGESTED MOTTOES:   Pray today.
                     The wings of prayer fly high.
                     Prayer: a conversation with God
                     Prayer moves the prayer.

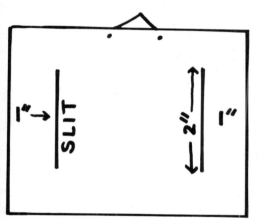  

Another way of constructing a frame is by using craft sticks. Using construction paper prepared as above, glue four around the edges of the front and four around the back. Print or type the verse or motto on a 2″ x 3″ piece of white paper and glue in the center of the 4″ x 5″ construction paper. Punch holes as above and insert a felt hanger.

SS845

# A BEDTIME PRAYER

Thank you, Jesus,
For stars so bright
That twinkle down
With cozy light.
Please care for me
All through the night.
Amen.

Fold a 6" x 12" piece of blue or black construction paper in half to form a "window." Cut out curtains, using colorful paper or fabric. Have children glue in place as shown. Attach prayer at bottom. Provide gummed stars to fill the night sky. The stand-up folder may be set by a bed as a reminder to pray before going to sleep.

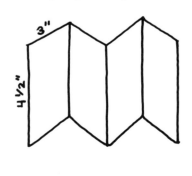

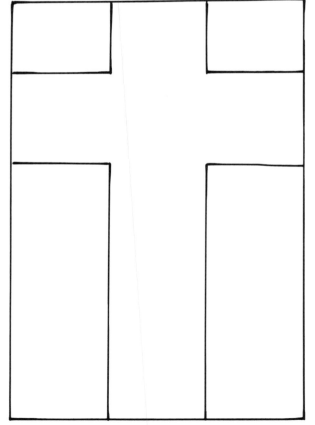

## A PRAYER FOLDER

Cut two strips of construction paper 4½" x 12". Divide into four 3" sections and fold as shown. On the second strip, cut out pattern of the cross. Unfold and glue the cross strip on top of the first folded strip. Write "PRAY WITHOUT CEASING" (I Thessalonians 5:17) on the cross pieces. Close and tie with yarn. Prayer folder may also be set up at home as a reminder to pray always.

SS845

# A PRAYER FLOWER

Many flowers close their petals when the sun goes down. Use this prayer flower to teach children reverence at prayer time.

For a more sturdy flower, glue pattern to construction paper and then cut out. Fold in along the dotted lines.

Show the children the prayer flower and explain how petals close at night. Tell them that this flower will be a reminder of how they should act during prayer. Demonstrate by saying, "First, we fold our hands (turn down petal); next, we bow our heads (turn over petal); and last, we close our eyes (turn over petal). Now we are ready to talk to God". Keep the flower closed during the prayers. At the conclusion, open the flower and thumbtack to a board or place in a special container. At each prayer time a child may be responsible for putting the flower away. Children may also like to take turns folding the petals and explaining how to be reverent. Make a prayer flower for each child to take home.

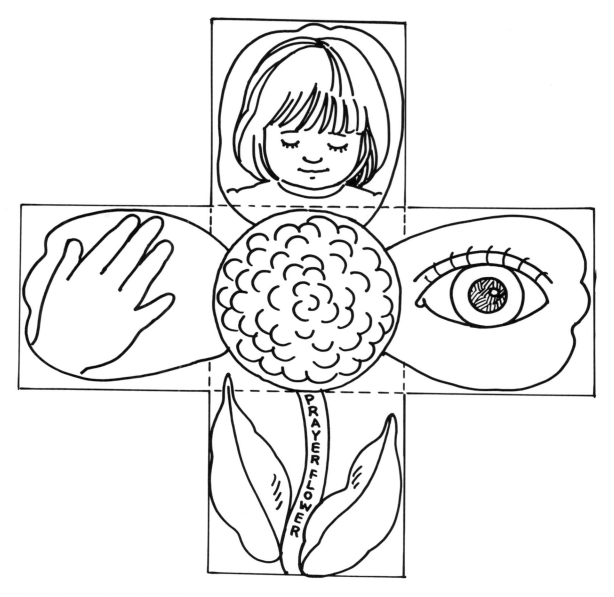

SS845

# THE NAME OF JESUS

In John 16:24 Jesus says, "Hitherto have ye asked nothing in my name: ask, and ye shall receive, that your joy may be full." These three activities stress the name of Jesus and may be used at any time during the study of His life.

## TOOTHPICK PRINTING

MATERIALS: colored toothpicks, glue, cotton swabs or small artist brushes, and construction paper.

For young children, print the letters JESUS CHRIST on a piece of construction paper. Have children outline each letter with glue, using a cotton swab or a small artist brush. (Glue may be dispensed on a small square of heavy paper or in a plastic lid.) Use whole and half toothpicks pressed onto the outlines to spell out the message. Older children may enjoy printing other words, such as "JESUS IS LOVE" or "KING OF KINGS."

1. *Christ*
2. *Good Shepherd*
3. *Lamb*
4. *Messiah*
5. *Saviour*

## BIRTH TO RESURRECTION

Cut a 4½" x 12" strip and divide into three 4" sections. In the middle print "JESUS." Provide Christmas and Easter cards. The children are to glue a picture of the Nativity on the left and a picture of the Resurrection (not the Crucifixion) on the right. Fold the left and right sections in, and print "THE MOST WONDERFUL NAME OF ALL" on the outside. The folder will stand freely when unfolded.

## HIS MANY NAMES

A concordance lists 102 names or descriptions of Jesus. Challenge older children to find as many as they can. Make a poster with numbered lines for the names and references. This activity may be ongoing. Encourage the children to use a concordance or Bible dictionary in their search. Younger children can be taught more familiar names: Christ, Good Shepherd, Lamb, Messiah and Savior. They can learn to spell them and to understand that they are all names for Jesus.

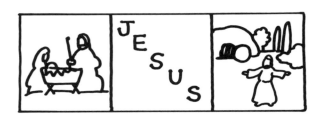

Shining Star Publications, Copyright © 1988, A division of Good Apple, Inc.

SS845

# WHERE HE WALKED

Jesus' ministry on earth lasted less than four years. During that time He traveled from place to place. He visited in big cities and rural villages. He taught in small synagogues and in the great temple. He walked the lands of Galilee, Samaria, Judea, Phoenicia, and Perea; but in that time He never ventured farther than 200 miles from where He was born. How wonderful that today His message of love has traveled all the way around the world!

SS845

# THE PLACES JESUS SAW

Unscramble the numbered cities and bodies of water on the map and fill in the numbered spaces below with the correct names.

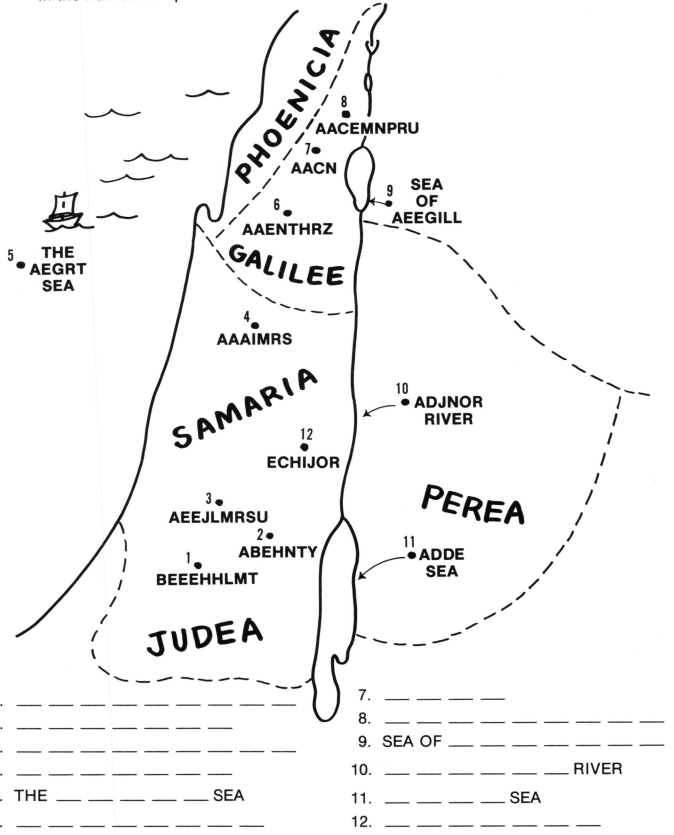

1. _ _ _ _ _ _ _ _ _
2. _ _ _ _ _ _ _
3. _ _ _ _ _ _ _ _ _
4. _ _ _ _ _ _ _
5. THE _ _ _ _ _ SEA
6. _ _ _ _ _ _ _ _

7. _ _ _ _
8. _ _ _ _ _ _ _ _ _
9. SEA OF _ _ _ _ _ _ _
10. _ _ _ _ _ _ RIVER
11. _ _ _ _ SEA
12. _ _ _ _ _ _ _

SS845

# THE SEA OF GALILEE

The Sea of Galilee is the scene of many of Jesus' teachings and healings. Help pupils to locate Galilee on a map. Explain that it is a freshwater lake surrounded by hills. It has been called a sea because of its great size. As in the time of Peter and Andrew, it is still known for its abundance of fish.

## MATCHUP

Using the pattern, cut out boats. On them print names of people that Jesus healed; the Disciples; Bible verses; persons in the parables; etc. Cut each boat in half and put sandpaper on the back of each piece. Put up a piece of blue flannel to represent the Sea of Galilee. As pupils arrive, pass out the boat halves. Ask them to find the person who has the matching half of their boat, and place the two pieces together on the "sea."

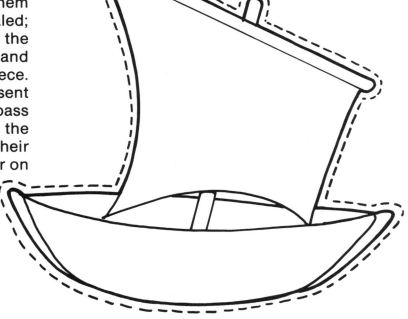

## SAILING THE SEA

Provide a small paper plate for each of the children. Instruct them to color the center blue. Give each pupil a walnut half, clay, a paper sail and a toothpick. They are to put the clay inside the shell and insert the pick with the sail attached. Pass out two short pieces of magnetic strip and a Popsicle stick. Direct pupils to attach one magnet under the shell and the other on the end of the stick. As they move the stick underneath the plate, it will cause the boat to "sail the sea."

Shining Star Publications, Copyright © 1988, A division of Good Apple, Inc.

SS845

# A MAP SEARCH

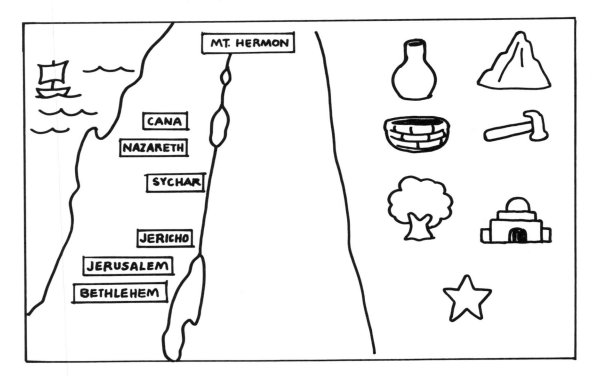

OBJECTIVE: To familiarize pupils with the places Jesus went and the events that took place there.

MATERIALS: Cover bulletin board with light-colored flannel. Using dark chalk, draw an outline map of the Holy Land, as shown. Print on strips of paper: CANA, BETHLEHEM, JERUSALEM, SYCHAR, MT. HERMON, NAZARETH, JERICHO. Glue sandpaper on the back and place each in correct spot on map. Cut out symbols on page 101 and glue sandpaper on back of each. Place on right side of board.

PROCEDURE: Give clues for each place and call on pupils to select the correct symbol and put it near the appropriate place on map.

MT. HERMON—The place of Jesus' Transfiguration.

NAZARETH—The place where Jesus lived and worked as a carpenter.

BETHLEHEM—The place where Jesus was born.

SYCHAR—The place where Jesus met the woman at the well.

CANA—Scene of Jesus changing water into wine.

JERUSALEM—Where Jesus often visited the Temple.

JERICHO—Where Zacchaeus climbed a tree to see Jesus.

The activity may be reversed by putting the symbols in the correct places on the map and having children select the right names and place them on the map.

SS845

# MAP SYMBOL PATTERNS

SS845

# IN THE SYNAGOGUE

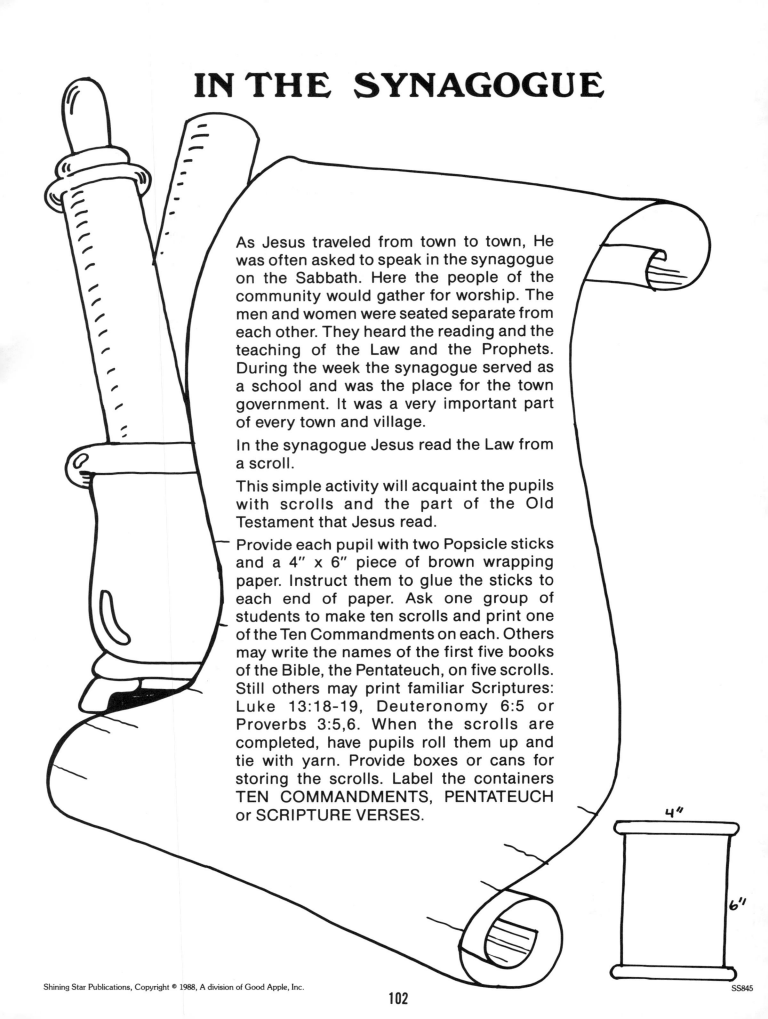

As Jesus traveled from town to town, He was often asked to speak in the synagogue on the Sabbath. Here the people of the community would gather for worship. The men and women were seated separate from each other. They heard the reading and the teaching of the Law and the Prophets. During the week the synagogue served as a school and was the place for the town government. It was a very important part of every town and village.

In the synagogue Jesus read the Law from a scroll.

This simple activity will acquaint the pupils with scrolls and the part of the Old Testament that Jesus read.

Provide each pupil with two Popsicle sticks and a 4" x 6" piece of brown wrapping paper. Instruct them to glue the sticks to each end of paper. Ask one group of students to make ten scrolls and print one of the Ten Commandments on each. Others may write the names of the first five books of the Bible, the Pentateuch, on five scrolls. Still others may print familiar Scriptures: Luke 13:18-19, Deuteronomy 6:5 or Proverbs 3:5,6. When the scrolls are completed, have pupils roll them up and tie with yarn. Provide boxes or cans for storing the scrolls. Label the containers TEN COMMANDMENTS, PENTATEUCH or SCRIPTURE VERSES.

4"

6"

SS845

# IN THE TEMPLE

Jesus made many trips to the Temple in Jerusalem. There, as a child, He answered difficult questions, and as a man he taught and fulfilled the law.

To give pupils a clearer picture of the Temple, make assignments for short reports. Topics may concern different parts of the Temple, or they may be answers to questions: What was in the Holy Place and the Holy of Holies? Who was allowed to enter each court? What happened in the Temple when Jesus died on the cross? Is any part of the Temple standing today? You may reproduce the diagram for each pupil to use in preparing his report. Provide Bible dictionaries and concordances. Give pupils an opportunity to share their writings.

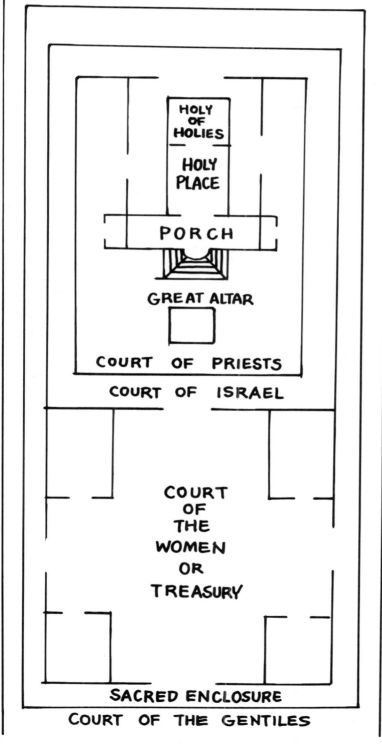

## MY REPORT

_____

_____

_____

_____

_____

_____

_____

_____

_____

_____

_____

_____

_____

_____

_____

_____

_____

_____

_____

_____

_____

_____

Shining Star Publications, Copyright © 1988, A division of Good Apple, Inc.          SS845

# TRAVELING THE HOLY LAND

This activity should help pupils to become more familiar with the Holy Land. Give each child a copy of the map on page 105 and the list of places with their color code. Make maps of the Holy Land available to the children. A large wall map would also be helpful. The pupils may refer to the large map while marking theirs. Instruct them to locate each city, country, mountain and body of water listed. They are to color the symbol and print the appropriate name on each map location.

**CITIES—YELLOW** ◯

Jerusalem
Bethlehem
Bethany
Jericho
Sychar
Nazareth
Cana
Capernaum
Caesarea Philippi
Gerasa

**MOUNTAINS—GREY** △

Mount Gerizim
Mount Hermon

**BODIES OF WATER—BLUE** ⊗

Dead Sea
Jordan River
Sea of Galilee
Great Sea

**COUNTRIES—GREEN** ☐

Judea
Perea
Decapolis
Galilee
Phoenicia
Samaria

SS845

# THE HOLY LAND MAP

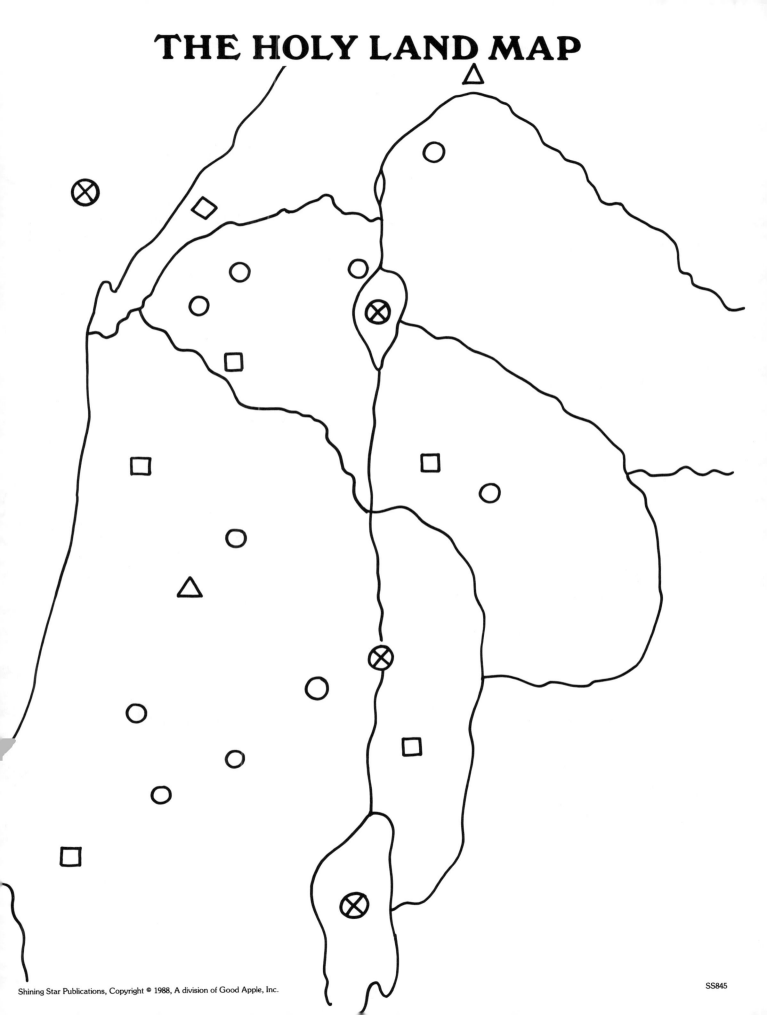

# TIME TO TRAVEL

## PACK YOUR BAGS!

Tell the pupils they are packing for a trip to the Holy Land. They are to take turns deciding what to take along. The items must be in alphabetical order and must have existed in Bible times—no airplane bags, baseballs or cameras!

You may wish to display the alphabet on a poster or chalkboard for younger children. They can look for items contained in teaching pictures or in Bible picture books. Older children will enjoy repeating all the items given and then adding their own choices. It is a real memory challenge. Then challenge children to unpack their bags by reversing the alphabet and naming items backwards, ending with A.

## FOLLOW THOSE FOOTPRINTS!

Use the flannelgraph map as described on page 100. Cut several footprints from the pattern and glue sandpaper on back of each. Draw a large X on a square of paper to which sandpaper has been attached. Choose a city, sea, mountain, etc., and place the X by it. This will be the secret spot.

Blindfold a pupil and spin him/her around. Point him/her toward map and direct the child to stick the footprint on the flannel, trying to place it as near as possible to the secret spot.

SS845

# A TABLETOP VILLAGE

Jesus visited numerous small villages when He traveled through the Holy Land. There the people came to hear Him teach or see Him heal the sick who were brought to Him.

Provide teaching pictures of street scenes and materials for the pupils to use in constructing a tabletop village. Tape a large poster board to the tabletop. The children may sketch a layout for their village. They will need to decide where to put houses, trees, a well, people, etc. Materials needed are small boxes of various shapes, clay, paper, glue, scissors, tree branches, pipe cleaners, paints, liquid markers and other odds and ends.

Mirrors may serve as water in the well. The well can be made of a cardboard circle or clay blocks. The pipe cleaners can serve as figures or as trees. If real sand is used it should be applied outdoors with glue, where the excess can be shaken off. When dry, the poster board can then be taped to the table. A green towel can be glued down for the grass. Be sure that one building is a synagogue. Small plastic animals may be included, or animals can be shaped from clay.

When completed, the city can be used as a backdrop in the telling of stories about Jesus. Following the instructions on page 32, the pupils may make stick puppets to be used in their storytelling.

SS845

# OUTDOOR ACTIVITIES

Why not plan to spend some quality time outdoors with your pupils? Here are some suggested activities.

## LET'S EAT

Plan a picnic that will include only foods eaten in Bible times—cheese, bread, dried fruits, fish, milk. This would be a good time to discuss what it would have been like to sit on a hillside and listen to Jesus teach, or to share in the miracle of the boy's lunch.

## MAP TAG

Before the children go outside, print the names of cities, seas, rivers, mountains or countries from the Holy Land on small posters and place on bushes, trees, sidewalks or buildings. Instruct the children that to be "safe" in this game of Map Tag, they must be touching a place from the Holy Land.

## ROUNDUP TIME

On trees, place posters that read "Disciples," "Christmas," or "Parable." Prepare signs to hang around pupils' necks. On a strip of construction paper print the name of a Disciple, a person in the Christmas story or someone mentioned in a parable. On the reverse side print another of those biblical names. Add a yarn loop to go around the neck. Give each child a sign, and tell him not to peek at the other side. At a given signal they will go to their posted places. All the Disciples will be together, as will all the Christmas people and all the parable people. Tell the pupils to turn over their signs and at the signal move to their new spot. Call children together to exchange their signs, and repeat the game.

SS845

# THE FINAL JOURNEY

Jesus knew His earthly ministry was coming to a close. The events of the last days lay ahead. There was the raising of Lazarus from the dead; His anointment with precious perfume; the triumphal entry into Jerusalem; the last Passover supper with the Disciples; the treachery of Judas; the agony in the garden; the denial of Peter; and above everything loomed the cross. Jesus knew everything that waited for Him, but still He did not turn from the path God had chosen for Him. There has never been so great a love!

# THE LAST WEEK

Complete the sentences and learn about some of the happenings of that most holy week. If you need help, look up the listed verses.

## SUNDAY

JESUS' ENTRY INTO JERUSALEM IS MET WITH SHOUTS OF

_ _ _ _ _ _ _ !

Matthew 21:9

## MONDAY

JESUS CALLS THE TEMPLE A DEN OF

_ _ _ _ _ _ _ .

Luke 19:46

## TUESDAY

JESUS COMMANDS THAT WE LOVE OUR

_ _ _ _ _ _ _ _ _ .

Mark 12:31

## WEDNESDAY

JUDAS ISCARIOT IS TAKEN OVER BY

_ _ _ _ _ .

Luke 22:3

## THURSDAY

JESUS HAS A LAST SUPPER WITH THE

_ _ _ _ _ .

Mark 14:17

## FRIDAY

JESUS IS DENIED THREE TIMES BY

_ _ _ _ _ .

Matthew 26:75

SS845

# EASTER BULLETIN BOARDS

OBJECTIVE: To guide pupils in an understanding that to follow Jesus means to put Him first in their lives every day.

DIRECTIONS: Cover board with blue paper. Reproduce child and Jesus and place top center. Cut out three "I's" and three crosses—small, medium, and large—and place as shown. Make letters, or print on the background "I WILL DECREASE" and "HE WILL INCREASE." Position under I's and crosses.

OBJECTIVE: To emphasize that the life of Jesus didn't just happen, but that it was a wonderful plan, willingly fulfilled by God's own Son.

DIRECTIONS: Cover board with white paper. Reproduce scroll, cross and heart with lettering. Ask children what each of these statements mean to them. For more color, flowers may be placed in corners.

# STILL HE CAME TO JERUSALEM
## Choral Reading
## by Lucille Golphenee

Provide real palm fronds or ones made of green paper, for some children to wave when the group says "Hosanna." Have the two solo speakers stand in the center of the group and step forward when they read their parts.

| | |
|---|---|
| FIRST SPEAKER: | The streets of the Holy City<br>Were lined with a great crowd.<br>They waved their palms and cried, |
| ALL: | Hosanna! Hosanna! |
| SECOND SPEAKER: | Jesus rode quietly among them<br>Sitting on a donkey.<br>The huge throng cried louder, |
| ALL: | Hosanna! Hosanna! |
| FIRST SPEAKER: | Jesus was the promised Messiah<br>Who would lead them in war<br>Against all their enemies. |
| ALL: | Hosanna! Hosanna! |
| SECOND SPEAKER: | The people did not understand<br>Who Jesus truly was.<br>They only knew to shout, |
| ALL: | Hosanna! Hosanna! |
| FIRST SPEAKER: | The crowd did not know the things<br>Jesus knew in His heart.<br>And, knowing, He still came. |
| ALL: | Hosanna! Hosanna! |
| SECOND SPEAKER: | Jesus knew that faithful Peter<br>Would deny Him three times.<br>Still He came to Jerusalem. |
| ALL: | Hosanna! Hosanna! |
| FIRST SPEAKER: | He knew that He would be betrayed<br>By Judas for some silver.<br>Still He came to Jerusalem. |
| ALL: | Hosanna! Hosanna! |
| FIRST SPEAKER: | Jesus knew that the cruel cross<br>Awaited Him on Calvary's hill.<br>Still He came to Jerusalem. |
| ALL: | Hosanna! Hosanna! |
| FIRST SPEAKER: | Does anyone wonder why He did it? |
| SECOND SPEAKER: | Why He chose to suffer so? |
| BOTH: | Because he loves you—that's why! |
| ALL: | Hosanna to Jesus Christ!<br>Hosanna to God's Son!<br>Hosanna to my Lord!<br>Hosanna! Hosanna! |

Shining Star Publications, Copyright © 1988, A division of Good Apple, Inc.

SS845

# BULLETIN! BULLETIN!

This activity will combine creative writing with the challenge of acting.

Instruct students to write short news announcements covering the days of the week before Jesus was crucified and the day of the Crucifixion: Jesus' entry into Jerusalem, cleansing the Temple, His arrest, the trial, His death, etc. Encourage children to use their Bibles for details. Begin each bulletin with "We interrupt this program to bring you the latest information about the man called Jesus."

Record music that the pupils will recognize. Make a radio from a shoe box, and place the recorder inside as shown. Make a microphone from a dowel and a small tin can. One pupil will be assigned to turn off the recorder and make the announcement to introduce each bulletin. The pupil will speak into the microphone and read the bulletin. Then the music will be turned back on. You may use this time to briefly discuss each event before the next bulletin comes in.

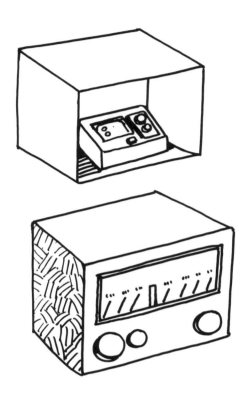

SS845

# JOURNEY TO JERUSALEM

As Jesus made His final trip to Jerusalem, many important events took place. This game will acquaint the pupils with those events.

MATERIALS:     Reproduce the game board on page 115, and cover with clear plastic or Con-Tact paper for durability. Make the spinner as described on page 68. Cut out 36 two-inch squares and write one letter of "JERUSALEM" on each square, making four complete sets. Place face down in center of board. Cut out the question cards below and also place in center, face down. Provide a button or other marker for each player.

PROCEDURE:     Instruct the pupils to take turns spinning the spinner and moving the number of spaces indicated. If they land on a 1 or a 2, they may draw that many letter squares. If they land on DRAW A CARD, they may take the top card and try to complete the sentence. If they give a correct answer, they will get one letter square and return the card to bottom of stack. If they are wrong they will return card to the bottom of the stack and wait for their next turn. The object of this game is to be the first to spell JERUSALEM with the letter squares. (Here are the answers. Teacher may keep these for reference. Lazarus; straight; Sabbath; one; children; riches; blind; Zacchaeus; perfume.)

| | |
|---|---|
| In Bethany Jesus raised<br><br>— — — — — — —<br><br>from the dead. | A woman bent over for 18 years was made<br><br>— — — — — — — —<br><br>by Jesus. |
| A ruler thought Jesus was wrong to heal on the<br><br>— — — — — — —. | Jesus taught that a shepherd searched for<br><br>— — —<br><br>lost sheep. |
| Jesus said the little<br><br>— — — — — — — —<br><br>could come unto him. | A young man would not give up his<br><br>— — — — — —<br><br>to follow Jesus. |
| Two men who were<br><br>— — — — —<br><br>asked Jesus to have mercy on them. | In Jericho<br><br>— — — — — — — — —<br><br>climbed a tree to see Jesus. |
| A woman anointed Jesus' feet with costly<br><br>— — — — — — —. | |

Shining Star Publications, Copyright © 1988, A division of Good Apple, Inc.     SS845

# JOURNEY TO JERUSALEM

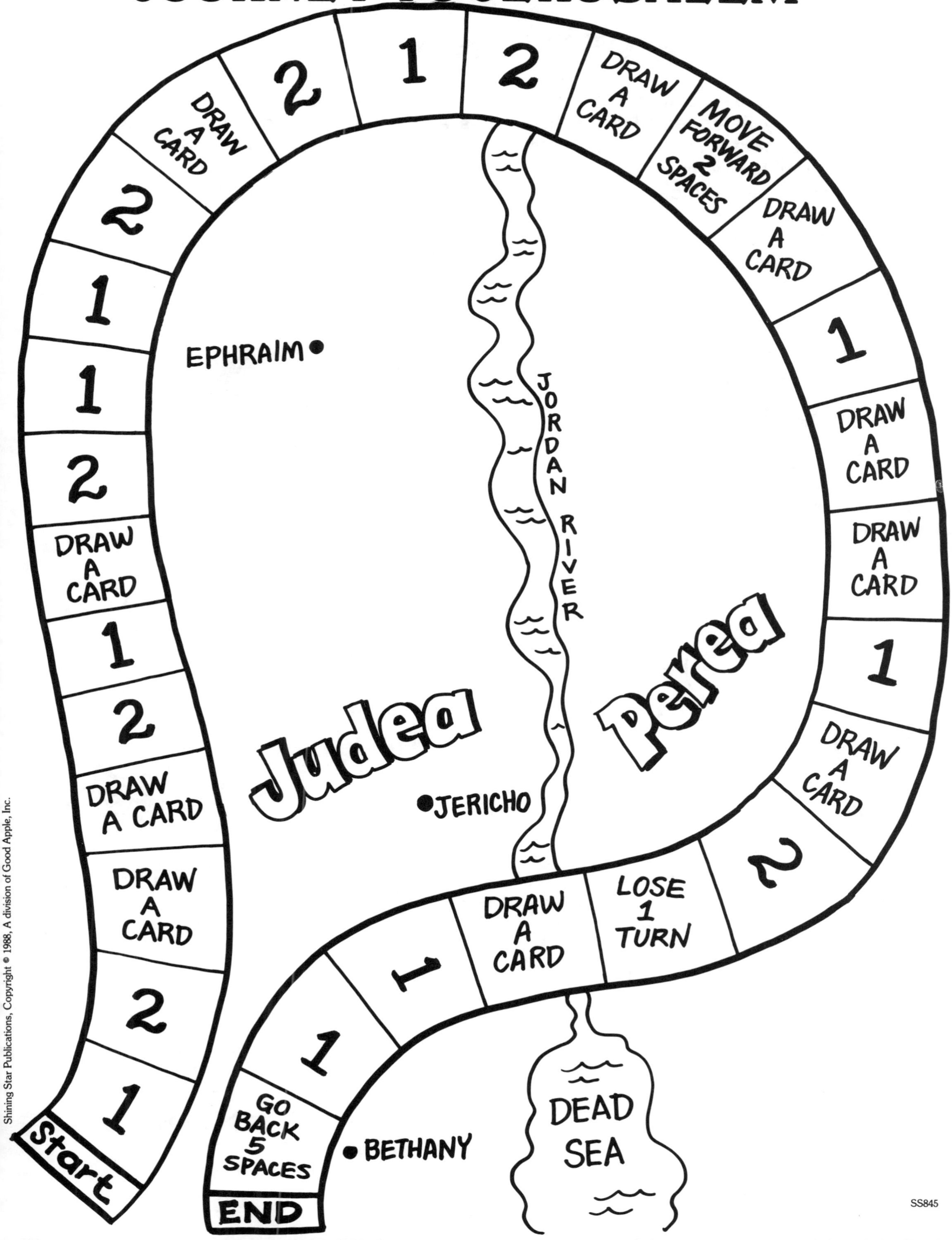

**Start**

1

2

1

1

2

1

2

DRAW A CARD

1

2

DRAW A CARD

DRAW A CARD

2

1

GO BACK 5 SPACES

**END**

DRAW A CARD

2

2

1

2

**EPHRAIM** ●

**Judea**

● JERICHO

● BETHANY

*JORDAN RIVER*

DRAW A CARD

MOVE FORWARD 2 SPACES

DRAW A CARD

1

DRAW A CARD

DRAW A CARD

1

**Perea**

DRAW A CARD

2

LOSE 1 TURN

DRAW A CARD

DEAD SEA

Shining Star Publications, Copyright © 1988, A division of Good Apple, Inc.

SS845

# PETER AND JUDAS

Two Disciples played important roles during the last days of Jesus' earthly ministry. Peter denied Jesus three times, and Judas betrayed Him. The pupils will benefit from comparing these two followers of Jesus. Reproduce the figures below on a poster. Assign half the class to study Peter and the other half to study Judas. Ask them to do a Scripture search on each Disciple and learn about personality, background, actions in those last days and what happened to them. A Bible dictionary can be made available. If figures are large enough, children may write their findings directly on them. If not, divide poster in half and leave space to write beside each figure.

SS845

# RISE AND SHINE!

Connect the dots to learn what sound saddened Peter when he had denied Jesus three times.

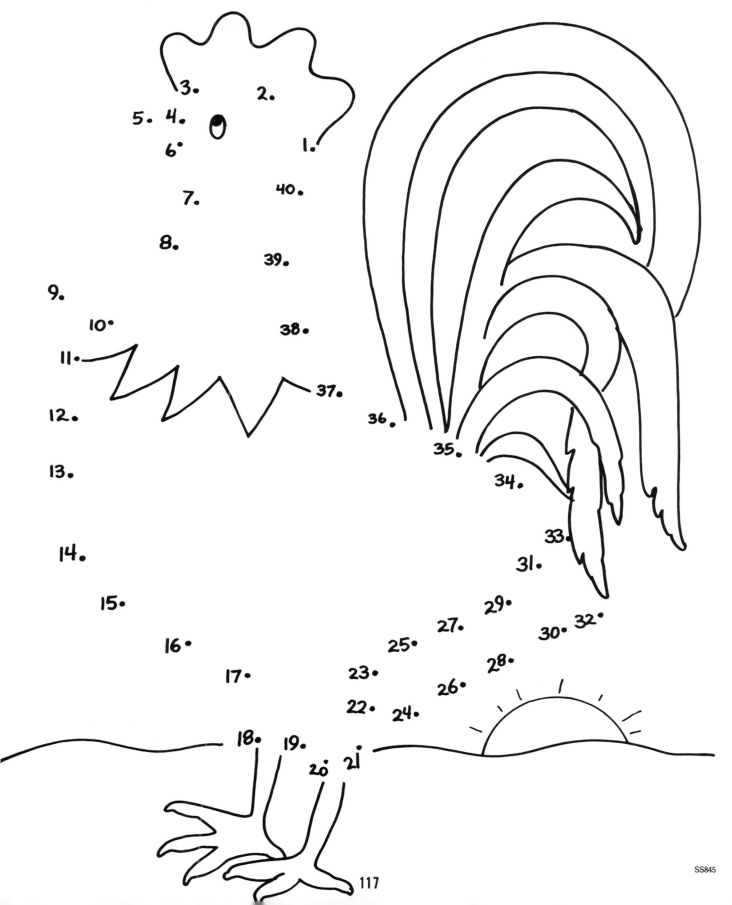

117

SS845

# JESUS' LAST SUPPER

This activity will help pupils to realize the significance of Jesus' last supper with His Disciples. Share the account of the first Passover from Exodus 12. Give pupils a list with pictures of the food eaten at a Passover meal. They may color them, and then cut out and glue to a round paper circle. Then read about the last supper of Jesus, from Matthew 26:17-30.

## WHAT FOOD MEANT

roasted lamb—symbol of God's protection and provision
bitter herbs—reminder of all their suffering in Egypt
unleavened bread—recalls the haste of their departure

## THE PASSOVER MEAL

Prayer
Cup blessed
Telling of first Passover
Psalms sung
Second cup blessed
Hands washed
Saying grace
Bread broken
Bitter herbs eaten with sauce
Roasted lamb eaten
Third cup blessed
Psalms sung
Fourth cup blessed

**UNLEAVENED BREAD**

**WINE**

**SAUCE**

**ROASTED LAMB**

**BITTER HERBS**

SS845

# DON'T MAKE A MOVE!

This is a version of the old game called pick-up sticks. Use ten tongue depressors or Popsicle sticks, and write numbers from 1 to 10 on them with a marker. Fold ten 3" X 5" cards in half and also number them 1 through 10. Print questions on each about the last days of Jesus' ministry. Place around the room.

Have a child gather up the ten sticks and then drop them so they are in a pile. He tries to pick up a stick without moving any others. If he can do this, he will then find the corresponding numbered question and try to answer it. If the answer is wrong, the stick goes back into the pile. If the answer given is correct, student keeps the stick. Continue until all the questions have been answered.

This activity can be used to cover any area of Jesus' life.

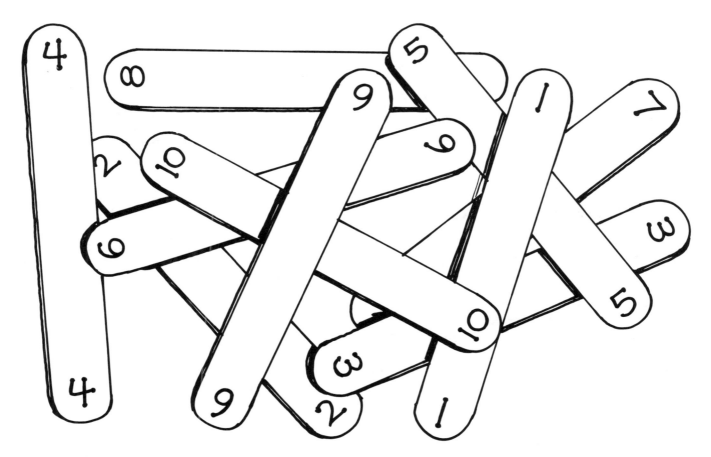

SS845

# MORE SEASONAL ACTIVITIES

## LEAVES OF SUMMER

Share Luke 21:29-30. Take pupils on a nature hike to collect leaves. In class provide clay, fine wire hairpins and waxed paper. Instruct them to make a clay circle or oval on the paper. Carefully press a leaf into the clay and poke the ends of the hairpin into the edge to form a hanger. Set aside to dry. Paint while leaf is still in clay. When dry, remove leaf. May be given as gifts to family, friends or shut-ins.

## THANKSGIVING THOUGHTS

Have pupils make a list of things they are thankful for. Read together II Corinthians 9:15. Ask what the gift is. Next, read John 3:16. Did any pupils include Jesus on their list? Pass out turkeys (see pattern), and direct children to write those things they are thankful for on the feathers. Place a magnet on backside and stick on refrigerator door.

## FEEDING THE FOWLS

Pupils will enjoy making a bird feeder to be used in the winter months. You will need a plastic jug, ¼" dowels, two screws and a piece of board to serve as a mounting. Cut openings in two sides of the jug. Punch out four holes for the perches, placing two of the opposite holes above the other two. Push dowels through the holes. Screw the jug to the piece of board. Attach to a tree, post or window frame. Fill with birdseed and watch the birds come for their winter feast! Read Matthew 6:26.

SS845

# AT THE CROSS

Jesus emerged from His time of prayer to face a mob and their ridicule. Ahead lay hurried trials, physical humiliation and the final steps to Calvary. Jesus knew He must fulfill God's plan and die on the cross. In that darkest hour His Disciples and loved ones were in despair; but soon that cross, the symbol of death, would become for all time the symbol of a victorious life!

SS845

# THE DAY OF THE CROSS

Find and circle the words that are related to the day of Crucifixion. They are hidden up, down, across, backwards and diagonally.

```
                    S A N N A R
                    E I H G I M
                    P I L A T E
                    U M I H I M
                    L A C R I B
                    C I N G O F
  G I S L E A R T H Q U A K E O C A L V A R Y
  S H A S T S E I R P O R L I E M I H E R O G
  I P I L A T H P E O C M E H P E S O J O H R
  M G O L G O T H A D A E I T V I E L O N C R
  O R A N L E O C R A I N U C A I A P H A S E
  N I C O D E M U S L B T O I W O M E N O A R
                    I N A S I R
                    L O R A N C
                    T R A O I E
                    E S B I H N
                    M O B E L T
                    I L A M N U
                    A D S E E R
                    H I M E N I
                    L E M O X O
                    M R R U I N
                    E S A O L D
                    L O G O D O
                    A I E M A N
                    S I N O R E
                    U R I E K A
                    R A V E N I
                    E P L N E T
                    J O H B S I
                    A L O T S G
                    A R I L M O
```

earthquake
centurion
Nicodemus
sepulchre
Jerusalem
Caiaphas
soldiers
darkness
Barabbas
garments
Golgotha
Calvary
council
vinegar
priests

Pilate
mother
Joseph
thorns
Herod
women
thief
Simon
linen
Annas
veil
John
lots
robe
mob

SS845

# JESUS' VICTORY
## Choral Reading
## by Lucille Golphenee

Divide the class into six groups. Within each group, change readers every two lines. You may want to alternate boys and girls.

GROUP ONE:
When Jesus traveled here on earth,
The Gospel He did preach,
And healed the sick, the deaf, the blind,
God's loving care to teach.
Many then believed on Him,
And tried to do His will.
But there were some who hated Him,
And sought the Lord to kill.

GROUP TWO:
When Jesus knew His time had come,
He yielded to their hands.
And one of His Disciples, Judas,
Led this wicked band.
They found Him in Gethsemane,
Where He had gone to pray.
Those evil men surrounded Him
And led the Lord away.

GROUP THREE:
Now, Pilate had informed the people
He would at the feast—
Whichever one that they preferred—
A prisoner release.
Then Pilate said, "Come, tell me now
Which one of them you choose—
Barabbas or this Jesus,
Who is called King of the Jews?"
The people were an angry mob,
And they, with one accord,
Cried out to save Barabbas,
And to crucify the Lord.

GROUP FOUR:
The loving Master suffered
Almost more than could be borne,
As they tortured Him and placed
Upon His head, a crown of thorns.
They led Him to Golgotha then,
And nailed Him to the cross.
He bore the sins of all the world,
At such an awful cost.

GROUP FIVE:
A most terrific earthquake came
When Jesus breathed His last.
The rocks were rent and graves were opened
By this mighty blast.
The people saw the blackened skies.
The awesome sights appear.
"He was the Son of God!" they cried,
And shook with anxious fear.

GROUP SIX:
A rich man, Joseph, took the Lord
And laid Him in his tomb.
There He was wrapped three days and nights,
In darkness and in gloom.

ALL:
But death could not contain Him long:
Our blessed Lord arose,
Triumphant and victorious
Over all His foes.

Shining Star Publications, Copyright © 1988, A division of Good Apple, Inc. SS845

# JESUS ON TRIAL

This play is to be presented like a Greek tragedy, with the actors holding masks in front of their faces as they speak their lines. Select pupils to be Caiaphas, Pilate, people in crowd, Barabbas and Jesus. Give each pupil a plain mask made from the patterns on pages 125 and 126. They are to cut out the eyes and mouth. Hair can be added with yarn, or may be colored in, along with eyebrows and a nose. The boys should attach the beard, and the girls should use the headcovering as part of their mask. Those playing specific roles will use the designated pattern for their headcovering. Tape a tongue depressor to the bottom of each mask to serve as a handle.

SETTING THE SCENE: Have crowd stand or sit, stage left, facing the audience. Place a table and chair stage center. Jesus will stand to the right of the table with his back to the audience. Actors will keep their masks up throughout the play.

# THE SCRIPT

Matthew 26:57-75, Matthew 27:1-26

(Caiaphas enters stage left and sits at table.)

CAIAPHAS:      I am Caiaphas, the high priest. I have come to judge this man who calls himself Messiah. Are there witnesses to this blasphemy?

(Two members of crowd step forward.)

FIRST:      We heard him say he would destroy the Temple and rebuild it in three days.

(Second man nods head in agreement and they return to crowd.)

CAIAPHAS:      Enough has been said. How do you find him?

CROWD:      Guilty! Guilty!

(Caiaphas joins crowd and Pilate enters stage left and sits down.)

PILATE:      I am Pilate, the governor of the province. This man was brought to me by your Council for judgment. I have questioned him and I find no fault in him.

CROWD:      No! No! He is guilty!

PILATE:      As is the custom at the Passover, I can release one prisoner. Bring out the thief, Barabbas.

(Barabbas is brought forward by two men. They stand stage left.)

PILATE:      Now, which of the two shall I release?

CROWD:      Barabbas! Give us Barabbas!

PILATE:      What then shall I do with this man? (Points to Jesus.)

CROWD:      Crucify him! To Calvary with him!

(Barabbas and the two men join the crowd.)

PILATE:      Then I wash my hands of this man's innocent blood. Do with Him as you will.

(Two men from crowd move to Jesus and take Him by the arms. They turn Jesus, and He faces audience for first time.)

JESUS:      I am Jesus Christ, the Son of God. This day my Father's will has been done. Now the cross awaits me.

     (Jesus is led off stage right, followed by Caiaphas, Barabbas and the crowd. Pilate stands at the table for a few moments watching after them. Then with head down, he exits stage left.)

# THE END

124

SS845

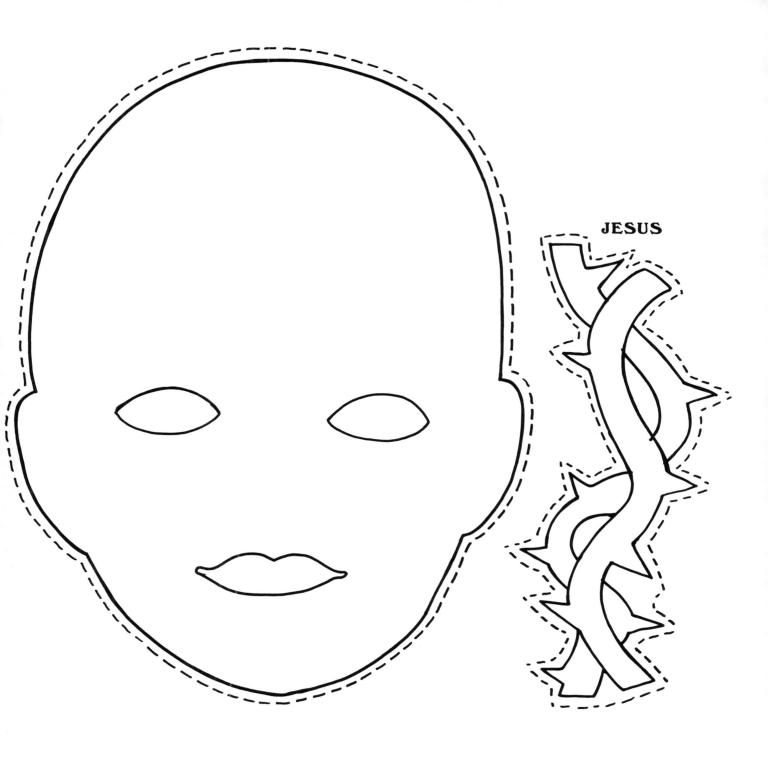

JESUS

PILATE

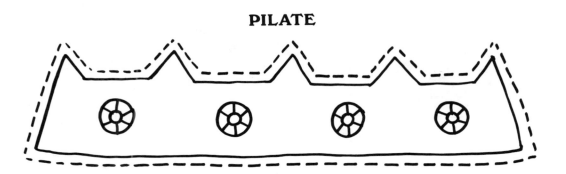

SS845

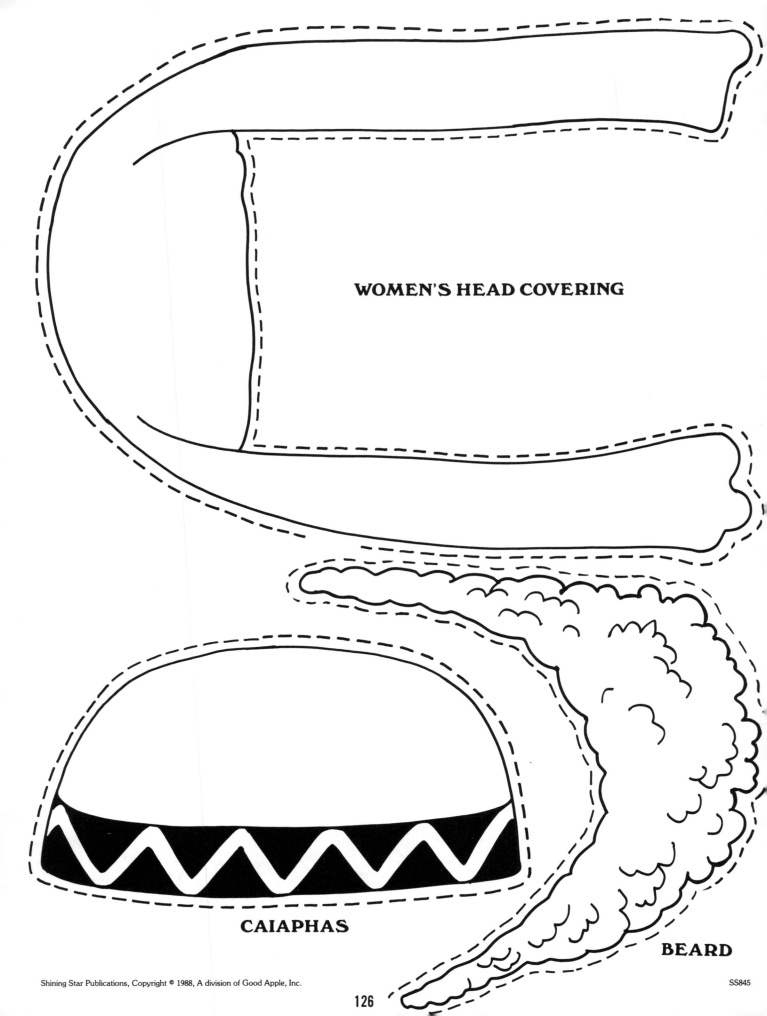

WOMEN'S HEAD COVERING

CAIAPHAS

BEARD

SS845

# EYEWITNESS REPORTS

In this activity the pupils will role-play people who might have been in the crowd that lined the road to Calvary. They include Mary, John, Simon the Cyrene, Barabbas, the centurion and Joseph of Arimathaea. Three pupils will be reporters: one from television station WJER, one from the newspaper *The Jerusalem Journal* and the other from the magazine *Roman Time*. Others may be photographers and a television cameraman. The television can be made from a box with a paper tube sticking out.

The television reporter can interview Mary and John; the newspaper reporter, Barabbas and Simon; and the magazine reporter, Joseph and the centurion. Let the three reporters work together in preparing their interviews. They will need to decide what questions to ask: What is the reaction to the trial verdict? Did anyone hear Jesus say He would come back to life? Who do they think He is? Where will they go from here? Etc.

After the groups have practiced, they may present their interviews to the class. Direct everyone to gather together as if standing alongside a road. The reporters may take turns presenting their eyewitness reports.

SS845

# WORDS FROM THE CROSS

Reproduce cross and cut into seven pieces, as marked. Number each one. Make three or more sets. Scatter all pieces around room. Divide class into the same number of groups as there are hidden crosses. Instruct each group to find all seven numbered pieces and reconstruct the cross on a sheet of construction paper. Spend time discussing what Jesus said and to whom.

⑤ I thirst. JOHN 19:28

⑥ Father, into thy hands I commend my Spirit. LUKE 23:46

① Verily I say unto thee, Today shalt thou be with me in paradise. LUKE 23:43

④ Father, forgive them; for they know not what they do. LUKE 23:34

② Woman, behold thy son! Behold thy mother! JOHN 19:26, 27

③ My God, my God, why hast thou forsaken me? MATTHEW 27:46

⑦ It is finished. JOHN 19:30

Shining Star Publications, Copyright © 1988, A division of Good Apple, Inc.

SS845

# THE THREE CROSSES

Jesus was crucified with two thieves, one on either side of Him. Three crosses were erected on Calvary. Cut out the three crosses below, using three different colors of paper. Instruct the pupils to put them together as shown. Tape a loop of yarn on back for a hanger. Add the words "Jesus Loves You." Discuss with children how the cross proves that Jesus loves them. Point out that as each cross is bigger than the next, so Jesus' love can grow in their hearts as they learn more about Him and try to be more like Him every day.

JESUS LOVES YOU

SS845

# ENVELOPE VIEWER

To make an envelope viewer you will need personal-size envelopes, scissors and crayons or markers. Give each pupil an envelope and a copy of the picture strips on page 131. For stability, the strips may be glued to strips of colored paper. Mark envelopes with the center square and side openings. Instruct pupils to cut out the square from front, then cut out side openings and seal the envelope. They may color the picture strips. Direct them to insert a strip into a side opening and push through until the first picture is in the square. Encourage children to tell you how each picture relates to the life of Jesus.

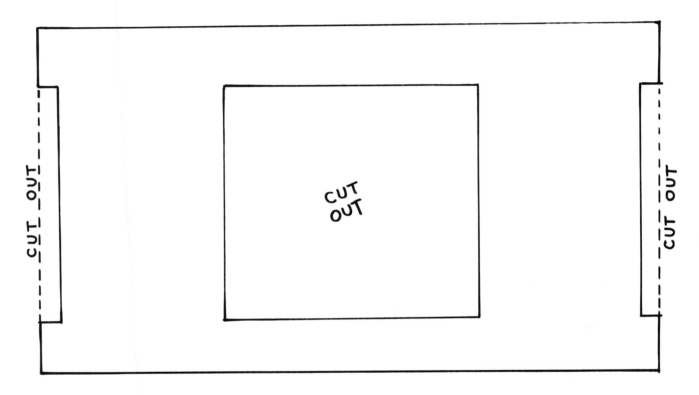

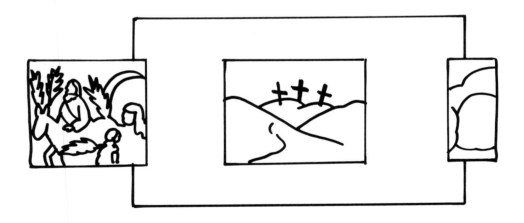

SS845

# PICTURE STRIPS

SS845

# TEACHING TIPS
## THE THREE P's

Every teacher, no matter how much they love to teach, can become tired and even discouraged with their tasks. Here are three "P's" that may help perk up your spirits.

### PATIENCE

Most teachers at one time or another experience discipline problems in their class. You may feel you need the patience of Job to act as a referee. Try treating each child as an individual. Seek to understand why he acts the way he does. Be firm and patient. The goal is to teach respect, not just blind obedience. It does seem that even the most boistrous children will learn, if the teacher persists with love and patience.

### PREPARATION

Many teachers are literally swamped. They lead active lives that include responsibilities beyond the classroom. Often the lesson is left for the night before or the morning of! You may get by, but consider how much greater the blessing would be for you and your pupils if you spent quality time in preparation. Thinking about the lesson days ahead of time can open your eyes to those things God may lay out before you to use. It can put an excitement in your teaching that is missing when you hurriedly read the Scriptures and pass out blank paper for the pupils to draw a picture on!

### PRAYER

Every teacher knows to pray, but often neglects to do so in the whirlwind of activities. Instead of waiting until you are pulling your hair out and stand in need of prayer, try to make prayer a daily habit. Each day spend time talking with God about your pupils, or the lesson, or anything else that concerns your teaching. Prayer is the best "perker-upper" a teacher can have!

SS845

# RESURRECTION TO ASCENSION

The promise of God has been fulfilled, for the Messiah has truly come. The babe born in a manger is now Savior of the world. Jesus Christ, the Son of God, has broken the bonds of death and has risen, just as He said He would. Jesus lives today, tomorrow and forevermore!

SS845

# THE GREATEST MIRACLE

Complete each of the sentences with the correct word.

Jesus triumphantly enters the city of    __ __ **R** __ __ __ __ __ __.

Judas betrays Him for thirty pieces of    __ **I** __ __ __ __.

Pilate condemns Jesus to die on the    __ __ **S** __.

A borrowed tomb is lovingly given by    __ __ __ **E** __ __.

The opening is sealed with a large    __ __ __ **N** __.

Jesus lies in the tomb for three    __ __ __ **S**.

Women approaching the tomb see an    **A** __ __ __.

The messenger shows them an empty    __ __ **V** __.

They hurry to report that Jesus is    __ __ **I** __ __.

He appears to the Eleven in an upper    __ **O** __ __.

They now believe that Jesus has truly    **R** __ __ __ __.

# CELEBRATING EASTER
## COLLAGES

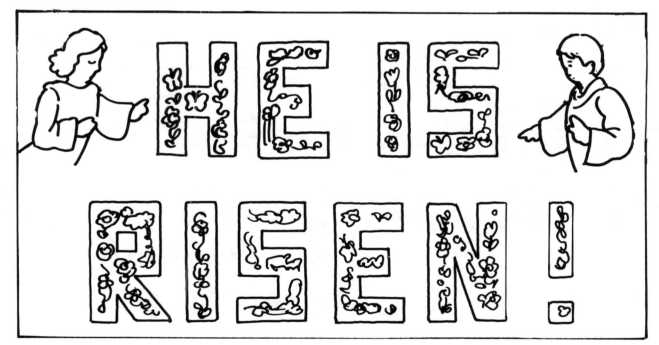

OBJECTIVE: To remind children in simple terms what Easter means.

MATERIALS: Pictures from magazines, poster board, glue and scissors.

PROCEDURE: Instruct pupils to make a collage of pictures on the poster board. Use pictures pertaining to one subject, such as nature. When the collage is dry, attach letters from the words below. Trace around them, cut out and pin to board, as shown. Figures may be reproduced with an overhead projector.

SS845

# HOSANNA!

## Words and Music
## by Helen Friesen

SS845

# SYMBOL OF EASTER

Jesus said that flowers remind us of the goodness of God. The white lily has become a symbol of Jesus' Resurrection. Legend says that its trumpet-shaped flower is a reminder of the good news heralded by the angels on that first Easter morning.

If possible have a live Easter lily to show children. Provide sheets of colored paper and glue. Give each pupil a red pot, brown bulb, green stem and white bud and flower. (Cut out before class or have pupils cut their own.) Direct them to first "plant" their bulb in the pot by gluing to the paper. Discuss what the bulb will need in order to grow. Next add green stem with white bud. Point out that the bud is the first sign of new life. Last, glue on the flower. Pupils may print "Happy Easter" on the pot.

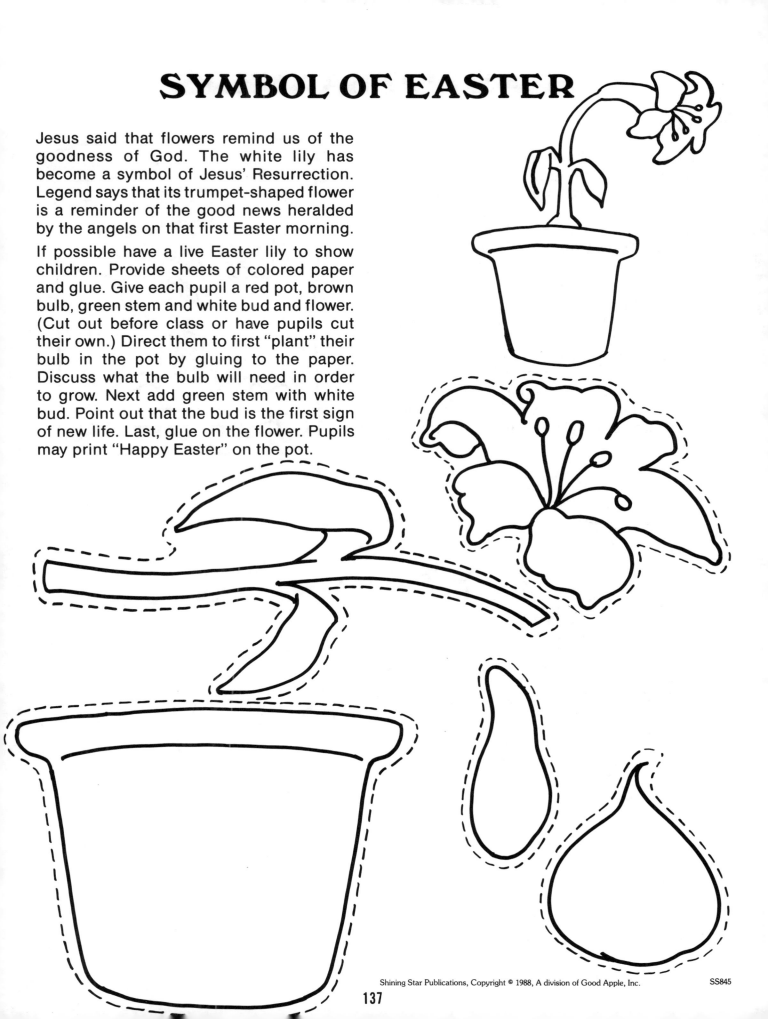

SS845

# EASTER BANNERS

These banners may be given as gifts or hung around the room. Give each pupil a piece of 8″ x 12″ solid-colored fabric or felt, a 10″ dowel and yarn. Direct them to glue one end of the material over the dowel and then tie yarn to ends of dowel to form a hanger. Provide patterns shown on this page and on page 139 for each pupil and colorful printed fabric or felt. Instruct pupils to pin patterns to material and cut around them. Glue figures to banner. The words "Happy Easter" or "He Is Risen" may be printed on white material with a marker and then glued to banner. Pupils may like to add fabric flower cutouts, using pattern illustrated or they may think of other trims.

# EASTER BANNER
# PATTERNS

SS845

# EASTER CARDS

Children will enjoy making and giving these Easter cards.

For the first card provide pieces of construction paper and foil cut into 3" x 4" pieces, glue, scissors, a marker and cotton balls. Use the pattern provided to cut a cross from one piece of colored paper. Glue it to the center of a piece of foil. Pull apart a cotton ball and glue it to the center of another piece of 3" x 4" colored paper. Glue it to the foil, forming a "puffed-out" cross. Print "REJOICE" beneath the cross.

The second card is a closed "Bible" with a cross-shaped bookmark inside. You will need crosses cut from colored paper (use same pattern as above), narrow ribbon, 4" x 6" colored paper, scissors, glue and a marker. Make slits in the cross, as shown, and thread a ribbon through them. Fold the 4" x 6" paper in half to form a booklet. Round off the cover edges. Print "Happy Easter" on front, and slip the cross-shaped bookmark inside. A "clasp" may be formed by gluing a narrow strip of paper on the center front of the booklet and a tab on the back. (See illustration.)

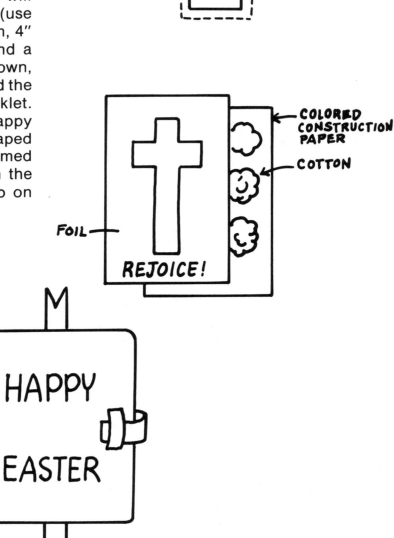

# THE GREAT COMMISSION

This activity will help pupils to learn Jesus' last commandment before His Ascension to heaven. Reproduce the globe patterns, making appropriate cutouts on the second one. (See below.) Go over the verses with the children. Explain that this is a call to action for the followers of Jesus. Cover the first globe with the second. Now only the action words of the commandment show. Ask pupils what these words are telling them to do. Uncover and again go over the verses. Give pupils an opportunity to repeat the commandment when they have memorized it.

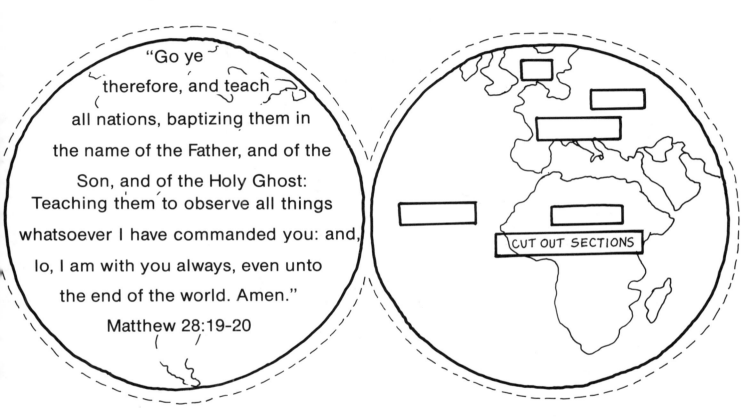

"Go ye therefore, and teach all nations, baptizing them in the name of the Father, and of the Son, and of the Holy Ghost: Teaching them to observe all things whatsoever I have commanded you: and, lo, I am with you always, even unto the end of the world. Amen."

Matthew 28:19-20

CUT OUT SECTIONS

## WHAT JESUS MEANS TO ME

Reproduce the picture of Jesus found on the following page. Instruct pupils to color it. Now that they have completed the study of the life of Jesus, ask them to write on the lines what Jesus has come to mean to them. This picture may be used to complete the book of coloring pictures that the pupils have compiled during the study.

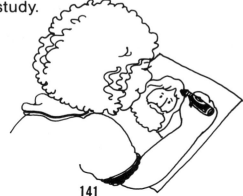

SS845

_____

_____

_____

_____

SS845

# ANSWER KEY

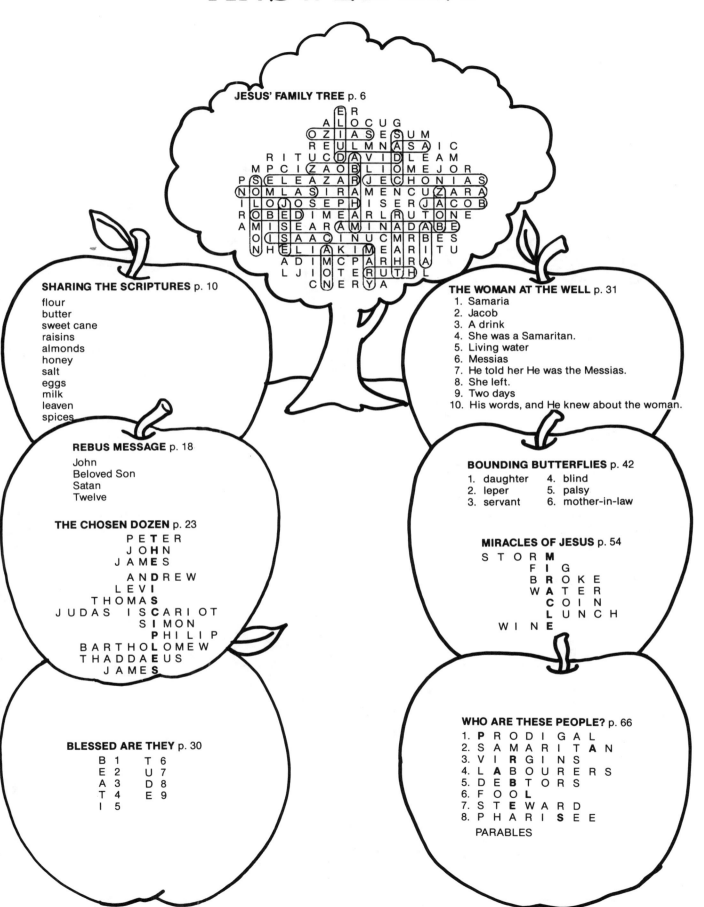

**JESUS' FAMILY TREE** p. 6

```
            E R
        A   L O C U G
      O Z I A S E S U M
        R E U L M N A S A I C
      R I T U C D A V I D L E A M
    M P C I Z A O B L I O M E J O R
  P S E L E A Z A R J E C H O N I A S
  N O M L A S I R A M E N C U Z A R A
  I L O J O S E P H I S E R J A C O B
  R O B E D I M E A R L R U T O N E
  A M I S E A R A M I N A D A B E
  O N I S A A C I N U C M R B E S U
  N H E L I A K I M E A R H R T U
      A D I M C P A R H R A
      L J I O T E R U T H L
        C N E R Y A
```

**SHARING THE SCRIPTURES** p. 10

flour
butter
sweet cane
raisins
almonds
honey
salt
eggs
milk
leaven
spices

**REBUS MESSAGE** p. 18

John
Beloved Son
Satan
Twelve

**THE CHOSEN DOZEN** p. 23

```
        P E T E R
        J O H N
        J A M E S
          A N D R E W
          L E V I
      T H O M A S
J U D A S   I S C A R I O T
          S I M O N
          P H I L I P
    B A R T H O L O M E W
    T H A D D A E U S
        J A M E S
```

**BLESSED ARE THEY** p. 30

```
    B  1      T  6
    E  2      U  7
    A  3      D  8
    T  4      E  9
    I  5
```

**THE WOMAN AT THE WELL** p. 31

1. Samaria
2. Jacob
3. A drink
4. She was a Samaritan.
5. Living water
6. Messias
7. He told her He was the Messias.
8. She left.
9. Two days
10. His words, and He knew about the woman.

**BOUNDING BUTTERFLIES** p. 42

1. daughter   4. blind
2. leper      5. palsy
3. servant    6. mother-in-law

**MIRACLES OF JESUS** p. 54

```
S T O R M
        F I G
        B R O K E
        W A T E R
        M A C O I N
        C L U N C H
    W I N E
```

**WHO ARE THESE PEOPLE?** p. 66

1. P R O D I G A L
2. S A M A R I T A N
3. V I R G I N S
4. L A B O U R E R S
5. D E B T O R S
6. F O O L
7. S T E W A R D
8. P H A R I S E E

PARABLES

SS845

**THE DAY OF THE CROSS** p. 122

```
                    S A N N A R
                    E I H G I M
                    P I L A T E
                    U M I H I M
                    L A C R I B
                    C I N G O F
G I S L E A R T H Q U A K E O C A L V A R Y
S H A S T S E I R P O R L I E M I H E R O G
I P I L A T H P E O C M E H P E S O J O H R
M G O L G O T H A D A E I T V I E L O N C R
O R A N L E O C R A I N U C A I A P H A S E
N I C O D E M U S L B T O I W O M E N O A R
                    N A S I R
                    L O R A N C
                    T R A O I E
                    E S B I H N
                    M O B E L T
                    I L A M N U
                    A D S E E R
                    H I M E N I
                    L E M O X O
                    R R U I N N
                    E S A O L D
                    E L Q G O D
                    L A I E M A
                    A S I N O R
                    S U R A N E
                    U R A V E A
                    R E P L N E T
                    E J O H B S I
                    A   L O T S G
                    A R I L M O
```

**OBJECTIVELY SPEAKING** p. 76

```
              P
    T A R E S E
  S E E D   A
  R         R
  E         L
  A             C
  S             O
  U         L E A V E N
  R             I
  E             N
```

TARES · SEED · LEAVEN · PEARL · COIN · TREASURE

**THE PRAYERS OF JESUS** p. 86

```
        B A P T I Z E D
        M O R N I N G
G E T H S E M A R N E
C A L V A E V Y
        E V E N I N G S
W I L D E R N E S S K S N
        C H I L H D R E N
              O U
        S U P P E R N T A I N
```

**THE LAST WEEK** p. 110

| | |
|---|---|
| Sunday | Hosanna |
| Monday | Thieves |
| Tuesday | Neighbour |
| Wednesday | Satan |
| Thursday | Twelve |
| Friday | Peter |

**THE GREATEST MIRACLE** p. 134

```
J E R U S A L E M
  S O I L V E R
C R O S O S P H
J S O T O Y S P E
D A Y O S A N G E L
G R A L R I V E M
  A   L O   O E M
  R     R I S E N
```

**THE PLACES JESUS SAW** p. 98

1. Bethlehem
2. Bethany
3. Jerusalem
4. Samaria
5. The Great Sea
6. Nazareth
7. Cana
8. Capernaum
9. Sea of Galilee
10. Jordan River
11. Dead Sea
12. Jericho